# THE PRICE
# OF LIBERTY

*EDITED BY*

ALAN REITMAN

———

# THE PRICE
# OF LIBERTY

———

*W·W·NORTON & COMPANY·INC·*

NEW YORK

# Contents

# Editor's Note

Knowledge and understanding of social problems are the bedrock on which constructive programs can be developed to help resolve society's ills. This is no less true in the volatile and complex area of civil liberties, itself a continuous swirl of controversy in the United States. This collection of essays was conceived for the purpose of shedding additional light on major civil liberties questions. By presenting the views of the expert-authors, it was hoped to stimulate further public thinking about these problems and to motivate the reader to personally participate in the continuing effort to preserve and advance civil liberties.

Not every civil liberties issue now confronting the ACLU and the nation is discussed, an assignment made impossible by limits of space and the speed of the rapidly changing civil liberties scene. The pace of change is so quick and the exigencies of publishing deadlines so demanding that in many instances primary themes rather than current factual developments are stressed.

The authors have shared common endeavors in the work of the American Civil Liberties Union and they often refer to specific policy positions. But the ACLU is the last organization to present a monolithic approach or "correct" answers. The questions the authors chose to discuss, and their views on them, represent their own separate, and quite individual, approaches. Where they agree with "official" ACLU policy, it is a happy coincidence, although not entirely an accident because of the important role the authors have played in shaping ACLU policy.

Whether or not they match the ACLU's position is of secondary importance. If their words accelerate deeper understanding of the civil liberties challenges of our time, both the opportunities and the potential disaster, and move the reader to recognize his responsibility to maintain and expand the institutions of liberty, the book will have achieved its purpose.

—A.R.

# Introduction

## by JOHN DE J. PEMBERTON, JR.

---

There are cycles in the development of civil liberties, just as there are periods of growth and regression in the life of a single individual. Right now there can be little doubt that in the United States our liberties have passed through a period of great growth, and may well be entering upon the wane; certainly they face a period ominously clouded by signs of regression. But there is much more to it than that.

The fluctuations of these cycles are, in the first place, related to external events. The thaw in the cold war, the burgeoning of domestic prosperity, and the seeming progress of the high aspirations invested in the civil rights movement provided a climate for the expansion of liberty in the early 1960's. Conversely, such recent threatening circumstances as war and the souring of the civil rights dream create a prospect of contraction in the immediate future.

The importance of the eight essays which comprise *The Price of Liberty* is significantly underscored by such portentous signs, for their authors' analyses help us understand how the main issues are influenced by such events. If the waning of the cycle leads to excesses—and one can scarcely doubt that it will—a firm appreciation of the merits of the main issues provides the first line of defense.

But the dynamics of change in civil liberties give this book an even greater significance. In addition to responding to external events, change of this order inheres in the nature and

9

history of this nation's institutions for the safeguarding of human rights. The commitments of the American Revolution and the erection of libertarian principles into constitutional guarantees gave a dual uniqueness to the position of individual liberty in the United States.

They first provided the business of liberty with a special place in the hierarchy of national values, as an end, or as the purpose of government itself. They made it incapable of being treated lightly as the mere by-product of official grace or benevolent rule. Thus the Declaration of Independence announced, after the invocation of such absolute rights as "life, liberty and the pursuit of happiness," that "To secure these rights governments are instituted among men . . . ." The history of the world and of the times contradicts an interpretation of this statement as an assertion of fact; it could have no meaning except as a declaration of national purpose. History has left this uniqueness of the American commitment relatively undisturbed.

The high station of liberty in the constellation of American values, moreover, gave the Bill of Rights a special place in the organic law of the land. It shares with other federal constitutional provisions a special status of superiority—through interpretation and application by an independent judiciary—to the acts of legislators and government officials who would otherwise have final say during their respective terms of office as to the content of the law or to the nature of its enforcement.

At the same time, this commitment and the erection of its principles into organic law in the federal and most state constitutions have saddled individual liberty with another kind of uniqueness in the United States. Liberty of this kind could not in the nature of things spring full-blown from the forehead of the Philadelphia convention. The compromises necessary to secure adoption of the Constitution, for one thing, precluded uncorrupted adherence to principle, and thus, the 1776 promise that "all men are created equal" came to be explicitly qualified in favor of human slavery in 1787. Similarly, the Bill of

Rights proposed by Congress in 1789 could not be made to govern actions by the states to limit, for instance, religious liberty or the enjoyment of the franchise by all citizens. What our forefathers had designed began, therefore, as a kind of Greek, golden-age democracy-of-the-elite, open only to those possessed of the requisite property, status, and creedal keys of admission.

The design, nevertheless, was written for *all* men, at all times, and here is the rub. From the beginning, our system promised more than it could deliver, and the promises came to be confused with performance. Never has the guarantee, "Congress shall make no law . . . abridging freedom of speech" been enforced in those absolute terms; yet every school child is taught that this is the fundamental law of the land. How easy it became to treat as actual performance the 1808 promise that no citizen (black or white) shall be denied "the equal protection of the laws"! In fact our history has been marked by an enormous (but always changing) gap between principle and practice in its protection of individual liberty and there can be little wonder that our children, educated by their participation in the civil rights movement in the early sixties, have come to regard that history as one governed by hypocrisy.

Thus the special quality of American institutions of liberty lies at once in their built-in mechanisms for self-perfection—the earliest efforts and greatest successes of the civil rights movement, for instance, were those which addressed the nation simply to obeying its laws, rather than to changing them—and in their capacity to camouflage failures. They sometimes respond well to determined efforts to eradicate excesses of repression and to bring about change, but they also tend to hide failures and encourage apathy and even cynicism. To the extent that the essays in this book equip those concerned with the merits of civil liberties issues to act effectively within such a setting, they are of timeless value.

The least discussed force, however, is that of the relationship and interaction between external forces which affect the state of our liberties and the internal dynamics of liberty's in- stitutions. In our system, constitutionally guaranteed liberties are not only an end in themselves, they are also a means to the end of self-government. Their actual enjoyment is not only affected by the successes or failures of society to resolve its most serious problems—national security, economic oppor- tunity, war, and educational opportunity—but they may be, and today they *must* be, used by that society to effect such resolutions. They are constitutionally guaranteed to make sure that they may be so employed, for they are often most des- perately needed at the very time when the intolerances of public opinion and officialdom most insistently demand their denial. The experience of the civil rights movement in the early sixties is again useful to illustrate this point. In this in- stance the means of liberty—the judicial processes and free- dom of expression—were conspicuously used to resolve a problem that was itself one of individual liberty, that of sys- tematic denial of the equal protection of law. The civil rights movement used the judicial processes to effect social change and peaceful protest and assembly to win adherents to its cause and, ultimately, to effect the passage of significant legis- lation. It experienced the harshest repressions of these liber- ties just as its substantive problem, legal inequality, had be- come most critical. And it invoked constitutional guaran- tees—with a fair measure of success (whenever resources were available to pursue legal remedies fully)—to defend its liberties from those repressions. A failure to deal with the problems of legal inequality by judicial decision and legisla- tion, then, would have saddled our social order with an explo- sive instability in which the liberties of no one could be se- cure, just as a failure today to resolve the problems of eco- nomic, educational, residential, and administrative inequal- ity—the legacy of legal inequality, as well as of racist preju- dice—threatens a similar volcanic eruption.

We *must* today perfect our liberties for use in the resolution of accumulating, unsolved social problems; our failure to do so will ultimately sacrifice the institutions of liberty themselves. One cannot imagine even-handed justice and respect for individual rights surviving the repressive measures, for which there already is an alarming clamor, that will be invoked in response to a now widely anticipated increase in urban violence. Thus far in the Vietnam war the nation has achieved a high score for protection of dissent as measured by experience in other wars and other nations. But that performance should not be expected to continue in the face of the anxieties which may follow serious military reverses or enlargement of the theater or the weaponry of the war. Harriet Pilpel amply documents the threats to privacy inherent in technology that is already in hand. It is unnecessary to tick off other areas of national life in which conditions not dealt with will end in the stifling of liberty. The meaning is too clear. Some of these conditions alone, and surely many of them in combination, if allowed merely to run their course, can quickly become too big to leave breathing room for the enjoyment and exercise of democratic liberties.

And yet we have moved too far in the direction of true self-government to be able to rely any longer on the unilateral actions of informed and wise leaders. A President may still conduct a war with divided public support, as did Lincoln in 1861–65 (that, however, was indeed a *civil* war). But it seems increasingly clear that neither the President nor any group of mere leaders can do that and at the same time commit an insecure people to those international bargains that may be essential for reducing the threat of nuclear disaster; to those domestic measures necessary for ending frustration and despair in our central cities; to those arrangements necessary for dealing with the threat of domestic and world famine; and to the host of uncounted adjustments required for making the era of electronics and computers one in which men may expand their horizons, approach realization of their visions, and control their technology in preference to being enslaved by it. Despite the proliferation of means of communication—in print and with electronics—we are failing to achieve that level of information and debate necessary to effective decision mak-

ing by a truly self-governing people. Indeed we have been
moving toward a dangerous polarization of blocs, in which
whites do not hear blacks, doves do not talk to hawks, and
neither facts nor ideas are communicated. Perhaps we are
using our mass media to communicate conclusions and epithets rather than information and ideas. Perhaps the defects
lie in the poor quality of our journalism and of our advocacy.
But I suggest that a more basic inadequacy is involved other
than the skill deficiences of newsmen, educators, politicians,
and lawyers.

That inadequacy lies in democratic perspectives—a consequence of deficiencies permeating the entire spectrum of
human rights, not merely those associated with debate and
the political process. The concept of self-government presupposes that men will assume some measure of individual responsibility for the actions of the community. Its premise is
that the subjects of government and the makers of its laws are
ultimately one and the same. There is no ruling class, for all
of the members of the society are at once its rulers.

But can a citizen of our commonwealth really be expected
to assume the responsibilities of rule unless the instrumentalities of government actually treat him as a ruler? The question may appear insignificant and obvious to a member of
today's urban (or suburban) middle or upper classes. The
officials of government with whom he has contact—internal
revenue agents, clerks and officials of administrative departments, policemen, his legislators, and, above all, the courts—
treat him with respect, if not always with courtesy and defer-
ence. They know his rights and they know he has the means
to assert those rights. But large numbers of people never see
the instruments of government in this light. To non-whites, it
is a grim joke even to suggest that the actions of the white
policeman (or the school administrator or the court officer)
toward them might be compared with those of a government
servant toward a member of the ruling class. To the poor, respect and dignity are remote from their experience with the
welfare department's administration—or with the administra-

tion of any other department of local government. Students, whether teen-age or adult, learn that respect for their full citizenship is often the last thing they will experience at the hands of school or university authorities. So long as officialdom itself shows contempt for the rights and liberties of individuals, it is foolish to expect those individuals to acquire the perspective that will encourage their exercise of such liberties in responsible participation in self government.

The inadequacies of our democratic perspectives are also observable with respect to the political freedoms. The provisions of the First Amendment, for instance, assumed that negative prohibitions on censorship would permit all information and points of view effectively to be introduced into public discussion. But this premise reckoned without present-day economic realities affecting access to such media of communication as printing and broadcasting. The proponents of unorthodox proposals for dealing with our novel problems face enormous odds against their being able to mobilize the financial resources and political organization necessary to afford them a serious hearing.

In short, for numerous minorities, whether defined by status or by political point of view, the democratic ideal has yet to come close to the point where rights and liberties are perceived as being available as instruments of self-government.

Attention to the practices of our society, more urgently even than to its principles, is essential for the reform of this void in perspectives.

At each level these essays speak of the dynamics of civil liberties; of the defense of these liberties against excesses of external forces causing change; of the employment of the American institutions of liberty for their own—always incomplete—self-perfection; and of the use of these liberties in dealing with the fast-moving problems of our times—for the sake of resolving these problems, and thereby perfecting and preserving democracy itself.

# THE PRICE
# OF LIBERTY

# I

# THE CHALLENGE
# OF PRIVACY

## by HARRIET F. PILPEL

Just as man, for the first time in the history, is capable—by nuclear fission—of destroying all life on eath, so today is he capable of destroying all privacy. He has it in his power, as the result of technological advance and unless he is restrained by strong doctrine and belief, to bring about Aldous Huxley's *Brave New World,* and worse—now. *1984* is chronologically and (potentially) technologically only a few years away. As George Orwell depicted that year, the western world had by then brought into being an era in which privacy had indeed ceased to exist. Those who read Mr. Orwell's book or saw the movie based on it will remember that a standard item in all dwellings was a telescreen by which "Big Brother was watching" all that went on in all the places where men lived and worked and played. At the time Mr. Orwell wrote *1984,* much of what he said seemed to be fantasy. Today, the wherewithal needed to accomplish the world he described and feared is in our hands and the only questions are when and whether we will use that wherewithal for the eradication of freedom and personal privacy. Perhaps "freedom and personal privacy" is redundant, for there is no freedom unless there is privacy.

Yet privacy as a right, as a civil liberty, is just beginning to emerge. And the word today means so many different and almost unrelated things that perhaps all that can be done in one brief chapter is to indicate what some of them are and where they appear to be going.

"Scientists," reported *The New York Times* on December 28, 1965, "must start thinking now about the possibility of mind control that their research may soon make possible." According to Dr. David Krech, professor of psychology at the University of California at Berkeley, "what our research may discover may carry with it even more serious implications than the awful, in both senses of the word, achievements of the atomic physicists."

Nor are "just" our minds likely to be under close surveillance. Some months ago, an appellate court in one of our western states held that there was no actionable invasion of privacy when government employees bored holes in the ceiling of a men's room in Yosemite National Park and looked down into the toilet stalls as part of a drive to detect homosexual behavior. According to the court, which held there was nothing illegal about this procedure, "the public interest in its privacy must be subordinated to the public interest in law enforcement." Apparently already today it is OK for "Big Brother" to be watching our most intimate function, at least in the private sections of places. A few months after the Yosemite case, an appellate court in Ohio reversed a conviction of a mother who, although warning her unmarried teenage daughter to stay away from sex relations, had told her—in their home, when they were alone together—that if she did not abstain, at least to make sure the boy used something— "rubbers." The mother's conviction was held to violate her freedom of speech. The case was also argued on privacy grounds. And, of course, several months before either of these decisions were reached, the United States Supreme Court had held that a Connecticut statute prohibiting the use of contraceptives infringed the right of privacy of Connecticut citizens.

Clearly, very different kinds of privacy are involved in these very different situations. But even taken together, they represent only a small part of the edge of the figurative iceberg of privacy. For example, at about the same time Warren Spahn, the well known baseball pitcher, was held, by the New York courts, to be entitled to damages and an injunction against the continued publication of a biography about him written for young adults. Because, said the courts, the book contained imagined dialogue and factual inaccuracies, it violated Mr. Spahn's right of privacy. Also at about the same time, the highest court of New York State held in *Hill* v. *Time, Inc.* that a *Life* magazine picture story comparing side by side the play *The Desperate Hours* and the family on whose actual experience it was said the play was based violated the family's right of privacy. (Incidentally, the author has always denied that his book was based on the Hills' experience but rather that *The Desperate Hours* was a composite of many different events. Both *The Desperate Hours* case and the Spahn case are discussed more fully below.)

While all these matters were under discussion—clearly reflecting the kind of things that were happening outside the courts—lapel microphones, closed circuit television in apartment houses and department stores, and electronic listening and viewing devices were, according to a nationally televised documentary (CBS Oct. 31, 1965), being freely sold and used without even giving rise to any significant court cases. We seemed to be taking them for granted as part of our way of life. And this taking for granted all the different kinds of privacy invasions in turn seems to be the result of a variety of forces to which we refer as "revolutions," and indeed, in a very real sense, that is what they are.

There is the psychological revolution. Until Freud there was little awareness of the psychological "innards" of human be-

ings, of the unconscious, the subconscious, the ego, the super-
ego, the id, or any of the other concepts which have truly
revolutionized our approach to people. We now have tests
and questionnaires used by government, businesses, schools,
and a variety of professional groups via psychiatrists, psychologists, and the like, designed to find out and make available
to other people things we don't even know about ourselves.
When, to these tests and questionnaires are added psycho-
therapy and psychoanalysis (undertaken, it is true, voluntarily
by the patient but certainly a "sharing" of privacy in a struc-
tured sense) and such phenomena as personality inventories
that are used increasingly in job finding, analysis, and evaluation, there is often little left of any individual's privacy in the
old sense of things that are just his own business, as it were.
Part of this, too, is the "revolution" in the treatment of mental
illness and emotional disturbance, the new drugs and techniques which condition men's minds and tranquillize them—
like Aldous Huxley's "soma" in *Brave New World,* the hyp-
notic murmur that conditioned its inhabitants as they drifted
off to sleep. These are not only not unbelievable today—they
are facts. There is also the technological revolution in the
development of surveillance devices and the development of
the welfare state "revolution" concepts which are discussed
below. And we must not forget the population explosion (or
revolution) and the polarization of our people toward the
large cities, which results in the lack of sheer physical space in
which to be alone. All of this, of course, pales into insignifi-
cance alongside the genetic revolution which, according to the
newspapers in February, 1966, was on the point of making
possible the breeding of babies outside the mother's body.
And finally, topping all this and making it that much more
pervasive, there is the "computer" revolution. Formerly, even
if things were known about people, even if they were subjected to surveillance and tests, it was not possible to latch on
to the information gathered in any massive way. It is getting
to the point today, however, where you may be able to press
a button and retrieve at one time all the previously gathered

data on the life and innermost thoughts of an individual. No matter how widely scattered it may be, we can increasingly, and as if by rubbing Aladdin's lamp, miraculously assemble such data quickly in one place.

As against this background, it is increasingly clear that some privacy rights simply must be, in the words of Justice Harlan, an integral part of our concept of "ordered liberty." If we are to so recognize them and protect them, it is essential we understand both what they are and against whom and what we are protecting them—the government, private individuals, or ourselves.

Important and provocative books have been and are being written on privacy in all its aspects—*The Naked Society* by Vance Packard, *The Privacy Invaders* by Myron Brenton, and the comprehensive study directed by Professor Alan Westin of Columbia University under the joint auspices of the Association of the Bar of the City of New York and the Carnegie Corporation, published in book form by Atheneum under the title *Privacy and Freedom*. All that a mere chapter can do is attempt to sketch in some of the desirable contours of the vital privacy areas.

Even if we attempt a bird's eye view of the right of privacy, therefore, we must, at the very least, divide it into three separate and distinct parts each involving basically different issues and constitutional choices: (1) the right of privacy viewed as the right to be free of surveillance, governmental and private; (2) the right of privacy viewed as the right to make the basic decisions affecting your own life without interference by the government; and (3) the right of privacy viewed as a limitation on what can be disseminated by the publishing and entertainment media.

*The right of privacy viewed as the right to be free of surveillance—governmental and private* / This is the aspect of the right with which *1984* is primarily concerned. And here we seem at times to be fighting a losing battle against big government, big business, and the apparently irresistible forces of technology. Concealed holes in the ceiling of a men's room is only a primitive method of surveillance compared with what science now makes available to us.

Minuscule electronic eyes and ears and other recording devices—lapel microphones in innocent looking brief cases and devices by which to hear both sides of a telephone conversation via a beam of light—are all commonplace today.

No one is safe from this kind of privacy invasion. On November 1, 1965, *The New York Times* reported that Mrs. Eleanor Roosevelt's hotel room was bugged during World War II so that "listening devices picked up not only telephone conversations, but also conversations in the room."

If this can and did happen to the President's wife, what chance have the rest of us got? Indeed, "Big Brother" *is* always watching. Many of these "bugging" devices can be bought for a small amount and used by anyone. Until recently the major brake on the endless proliferation of listening and viewing devices came via the laws against wire tapping and the much to be applauded regulations of the Federal Communications Commission under the Chairmanship of E. William Henry promulgated in early 1966. The regulations, explicitly couched in privacy terms, prohibit the indiscriminate use of mechanisms which use radio frequencies for transmission. But, of course, the FCC has no jurisdiction over other kinds of recording and transmitting contraptions. Only a few states have laws governing the use of other listening and looking devices. One of these states is Illinois (which has also taken the lead in another privacy area, sex offenses, by being the only state up to mid-1966 to substantially enact into law the Model Penal Code of the American Law Institute). The Illinois law applies to "any device capable of being used to hear or record oral conversation, whether such conversation is conducted in person, by telephone, or by any other means . . . ." (Radio, television, and, in general, communications to which the FCC regulations are applicable, are exempted from the Illinois law.)

Many intelligent arguments can be and are made for the

unrestricted use of these "Big Brother" watching and listening techniques. Most of them appear to be unimportant compared to the terrible invasion of privacy involved. What does seem clear is that we are only now beginning to pay attention to this whole area of privacy rights. Technology has advanced to a point where the failure of the government to take affirmative action against the use of "Big Brother" devices could have the same practical effect as if the government sanctioned their use. While legislation does exist against wire tapping (i.e. of telephone conversations) how much more dangerous is the use of recording equipment—visual and auditory—in private homes, offices, and stores. Just as many are questioning—especially since President Kennedy's assassination—whether just anyone should be able to buy a rifle, so we should be and to some extent are questioning the general availability of "bugging" devices and the old-line legal distinctions which would not prohibit their use except where they involved a physical trespass or a violation of a confidential relationship. While in Mr. Orwell's *1984* it was the government's use of these devices that destroyed all privacy, the destruction can become no less complete if the government leaves this whole question to property owners, employers, store keepers, and others who are motivated by their desire to prevent financial losses (what about insurance?) no matter what cost in privacy to the population as a whole. It is no one situation that matters. It is a cumulative effect.

Just the other day a person in a responsible editorial position with a responsible magazine publisher suggested that he and I continue on the street a conversation we were having in his office. "At least there," he said, "I doubt that anyone could pick up what we're saying." If this becomes endemic—if all of us feel we are being looked at and listened to wherever we are—free communication and action will become as impossible as if the government itself were doing the watching. Study and legislation are urgently needed in the nongovernmental area of privacy invasion. For at least where the government is involved, we are able to apply the constitutional

guarantees of the Fourth, Fifth, and Fourteenth Amendments.
And the United States Supreme Court and other courts, as
well as Attorney General Ramsay Clark, are now trying to
draw the guidelines. In mid-1967, the situation dealing with
areas not covered by the FCC appeared to be improving although there is still considerable confusion and lack of applicable or united doctrine regarding nongovernmental en-
croachments on privacy. As suggested above, the situation
could indeed develop to the point where the government's
failure to act to prevent private eavesdropping and bugging
might be regarded in itself as a governmental sanctioning of
all pervasive interferences with privacy. In fact, such governmental *nonaction* could be regarded as a violation of basic
constitutional guarantees. In any event, whether it is the government or a private group that is "watching" us, the destruction of our privacy can be the same.

But on the "official front" considerable progress was made
in 1967 as reported in an article appearing in *The New York
Times* for Friday, July 7, 1967, entitled "A Sweeping Ban on
Wiretapping Set for U.S. Aides: Attorney General's Rules Also
Bar Most Bugging Except in Security Cases." Attorney General Ramsay Clark's memorandum on the new regulations limiting wiretapping and electronic eavesdropping by Federal
agents is a major step forward. So is the United States Supreme Court's decision dealing with the validity of "New
York's permissive eavesdrop statute." It was charged that "the
statute sets up a system of surveillance which involves trespassory intrusions into private, constitutionally protected
premises, authorizes 'general searches' for 'mere evidence,' and
is an invasion of the privilege against self-incrimination." The
New York courts upheld the statute. The United States Supreme Court "concluded that the language of New York's
statute is too broad in its sweep resulting in a trespassory intrusion into a constitutionally protected area and is, therefore,
violative of the Fourth and Fourteenth Amendments."

Although the United States Supreme Court in invalidating

the New York statute did not face the question whether the press is precluded in any way from printing material obtained as the result of an invalid "bug," much of what it had to say on the subject has clear implications for the press.

The Court summed up the law saying, "In sum, it is fair to say that wiretapping on the whole is outlawed, except for permissive use by law enforcement officials in some States; while electronic eavesdropping is—save for seven States—permitted both officially and privately. And, in six of the seven States electronic eavesdropping ('bugging') is permissible on court order."

The Court put its finger on this basic twentieth-century problem of privacy when it said, "The law, though jealous of individual privacy, has not kept pace with these advances in scientific knowledge."

And the opinion referred back to a much earlier case that arose in a very different context where an earlier United States Supreme Court had said: "The principles . . . affect the very essence of constitutional liberty and security. They reach farther than the concrete form of the case . . . they apply to all invasions on the part of government and its employees of the sanctity of a man's home and the privacies of life."

The Court concluded that "few threats to liberty exist which are greater than that posed by the use of eavesdropping devices." Here Mr. Justice Douglas concurred and put the matter in the most concrete terms:

If a statute were to authorize placing a policeman in every home or office where it was shown that there was probable cause to believe that evidence of crime would be obtained, there is little doubt that it would be struck down as a bald invasion of privacy, far worse than the general warrents prohibited by the Fourth Amendment. I can see no difference between such a statute and one authorizing electronic surveillance which, in effect, places

an invisible policeman in the home. If anything, the latter
is more offensive because the homeowner is completely
unaware of the invasion of privacy.

Here too a number of judges separately concurred or dis-
sented. None of them really faced up to the question still in
invisible ink on the wall: Granting that either in general or altogether the use of wiretapping and electronic snooping and
eavesdropping is illegal, should it also be illegal to publish the
results of such activities? Think carefully before you even try
to answer that question for the consequences both ways are
grave. If the answer is "Yes, it should be" there is still another
legally imposed restriction on freedom of expression. If the
answer is "No, it should not be" then the privacy protection
resulting even from the strictest laws may prove illusory indeed. For even if a man can't be *convicted,* let's say, in a
court on the basis of evidence obtained by illegal electronic
snooping, how will he fare if the facts derived from the
snooping can nonetheless be made generally known? The recent developments and decisions in the libel and privacy fields
have a bearing here but they are not conclusive, for the material obtained from the "snooping" may be public in character
(so in that sense not really a privacy issue) and it may be—in
fact, by definition is almost certain to be—true (so that no
libel or privacy problem would be involved).

Justice Black, dissenting in this New York "snooping" case,
doesn't apparently see it as a freedom of expression problem
at all but one primarily of law enforcement.

As far as one can see, the argument has not yet been faced
either, which would go something to the effect that free
speech isn't free in today's world unless you have laws preventing electronic snooping and listening (which certainly is
the most effective deterrent to freedom of expression).

We conclude these as yet unanswerable questions by quoting Justice Douglas again:

In short, I do not see how any electronic surveillance that
collects evidence or provides leads to evidence is or can

be constitutional under the Fourth and Fifth Amendments. We could amend the Constitution and so provide a step that would take us closer to the ideological group we profess to despise. Until the amending process ushers us into that kind of totalitarian regime, I would adhere to the protection of privacy which the Fourth Amendment, fashioned in Congress and submitted to the people, was designed to afford the individual. And unlike my Brother Black, I would adhere to *Mapp* v. *Ohio*, 367 U.S. 643, and apply the exclusionary rule in state as well as Federal trials— a rule fashioned out of the Fourth Amendment and constituting a high constitutional barricade against the intrusion of Big Brother into the lives of us all.

*The Right of Privacy Viewed as the Right to Make the Basic Decision Affecting Your Own Life without Interference by the Government* / This aspect of "the right of privacy" is brand new as a declared constitutional right. It was first established by the United States Supreme Court in the Connecticut birth control case in June, 1965. Justice Goldberg, concurring with the majority opinion, described it as a "fundamental personal right, emanating 'from the totality of the constitutional scheme under which we live.'" Justice Harlan, in his concurring opinion, described it as an essential part of "the concept of ordered liberty."

The Court, in upholding this new privacy right, was talking about the right to use contraceptives and invalidated as an invasion of this right a Connecticut statute forbidding that use. It is ironic that at the same time other states like Mississippi and Virginia saw statutes introduced into, but not passed by, their legislatures which would have required people on pain of criminal penalty or denial of funds to use contraceptive measures. Justice Goldberg, in his concurring opinion in the Connecticut case, characterized *any* government interference, pro or con, with the right to decide whether and when to have children as "totalitarian" and "at complete variance with our constitutional concepts."

It is clear that the right of privacy in the sense of the right to be free of governmental dictation of the personal choices, which every human being in a democracy has a right to make for himself, goes far beyond the realm of birth control and has a special impact on that part of our population which is dependent on the government for all or part of its subsistence.

Until recently, little attention has been paid—certainly in terms of possible constitutional rights—to what Professor Charles Reich of the Yale Law School has called "a bill of rights for the disinherited." As Professor Reich points out in his brilliant article in the *Yale Law Journal* for June, 1965, entitled "Individual Rights and Social Welfare: The Emerging Legal Issues," the poverty group is an inevitable part of the kind of society we live in and those in this group are "entitled" to the same constitutional rights as the rest of our population. Professor Reich says:

> Perhaps, at one time we could have justified . . . discrimination against the poor by arguing that the poor are to be blamed for their poverty. But today we see poverty as the consequence of large impersonal forces in a complex industrial society—forces like automation, lack of jobs and changing technologies that are beyond the control of the individuals. It is closer to the truth to say that the poor are affirmative contributors to today's society, for we are organized as virtually to compel this sacrifice by a segment of our population. Since the enactment of the Social Security Act, we have recognized that they have a right—not a mere privilege—to a minimal share in the commonwealth.

This concept of "entitlement" is as yet barely rooted in our law—certainly not as a constitutional right. Professor Norman Dorsen's Project on Social Welfare at New York University Law School is very much concerned with this. As one of the leading appellate judges in New York (Judge Charles Breitel) put it, "A social welfare state by its very intrusiveness into all man's needs endangers his freedom and his privacy as much as any tyranny except that it is done in the name and fact of his own good. Naturally, a welfare recipient will have less to say about how he lives than one who pays his own way." Only the poor—those dependent on public agencies—are hurt by such a law as Connecticut's forbidding the use of contraceptives. The most effective and satisfactory contraceptives are, of course, those that require a doctor's prescription (i.e. the so called birth control pills and diaphragm) or insertion by a doctor (i.e. the intrauterine devices). The middle and upper income groups in Connecticut had no difficulty obtaining the necessary prescriptions or care from their private physicians—and they could, of course, always go to other states. But the part of the population which depends on public clinics couldn't get prescription contraceptives at all because there were no public clinics in hospitals or elsewhere which gave any contraceptive services.

The poor are also disadvantaged in many other aspects of their lives which fall within what should be a constitutionally guaranteed "zone of privacy." We have all read of the "midnight raids" conducted by welfare authorities on the homes of recipients of Aid to Dependent Children to make sure there is no man in the house: no constitutional right of privacy has as yet been established by the U.S. Supreme Court in such a context. In Alameda County, California, a midnight raid was conducted on the homes of five hundred mothers receiving ADC assistance. In Cook County, Illinois, one mother was refused aid because a case worker found a man's jacket in a closet in her apartment. It is unthinkable in 1966—and, one hopes, will be in 1984—that the population as a whole could be subjected to such searches for any cause whatever without a warrant issued pursuant to the now rather stringent rules dealing with search and seizure. Should the poor have any different or fewer constitutional rights? And recent court decisions and department rulings are now beginning to recognize that privacy belongs as a constitutional right to those who are dependent on welfare equally with those who are not.

Or, to take a less extreme example than the midnight raids—now judicially condemned in California. In the family planning field, the OEO at one time promulgated regulations setting forth conditions under which local communities may use poverty funds to make family planning services available. They were conditions which no one suggested should be imposed on the rest of the population in connection with their getting family supplies and services. However, the OEO has shown itself responsive to the arguments against some of the antiprivacy restraints it first imposed in connection with its family planning programs so that today the trend is in the direction of making services available on a basis which will not cut the basic privacy rights of those who look to public facilities for the means of exercising their family planning rights.

Examples can be multiplied. Under some state and local laws, now under widespread constitutional attacks (many of them successful), a man can be "punished" as a vagrant if he doesn't have a job. Again quoting Justice Douglas:

> Better that we be rid of the ancient poor laws that oppress our people, better that we outlaw arrests on "suspicion" and "without probable cause" . . . than that we reach the moon. Conquering of space has glamour and glitter, and it will be tremendously important in future centuries. But we live on earth; and here we will remain—at least most of us. It is what takes place in this block and in this neighborhood that gives the true reading on the health of our democratic way of life and on the actual vigor of our Bill of Rights.

With reference to both of these aspects, the all-important question arises as to whether the government, under our Constitution today, is mandated simply not to restrict constitutional freedom by governmental action, or whether it has an affirmative obligation to make possible the exercise of constitutional guarantees which the circumstances of the lives of many people make basically meaningless in the absence of governmental intervention.

Thus far we have at least given a bird's eye view first of the right of privacy in the sense of freedom from surveillance, governmental and private, and, second, in relation to the right of free men in a free society to make decisions in their own personal lives without being told by government what they may or may not decide. We come now to a third aspect—the aspect which until recently was the only one referred to as "the right of privacy"—namely, the right to be free of exploitation by the public media of expression and communication.

*The Right of Privacy Viewed as a Limitation on the Publishing and Entertainment Media* / We now come to the traditional (in this country) meaning of "the right of privacy" which has nothing to do with "Big"—or even "Little"—"Brother" surveillance or interference with personal decisions about one's own personal life.

In this country the recognition of a right of privacy was first called for by Justice (then Professor) Louis Dembitz Brandeis in an article co-authored by Samuel Warren in the 1890 *Harvard Law Review* entitled "The Right of Privacy." It is clear that what Brandeis and Warren were concerned about was the press. They expressed their concern in words which seem far more applicable today than one can imagine them being at the time they were uttered.

Recent inventions and business methods call attention to the next step which must be taken for the protection of the person and for securing to the individual . . . the right "to be let alone." Instantaneous photographs and newspaper enterprise have invaded the sacred precincts of private and domestic life, and numerous mechanical devices threaten to make good the prediction that "what is whispered in the closet shall be proclaimed from the housetops." . . . The press is overstepping in every direction the obvious bounds of propriety and decency. Gossip is no longer the resource of the idle rich and of the vicious, but has become a trade which is pursued with industry as well as effrontery. To satisfy a prurient taste, the details of sexual relations are spread, broadcast in the columns of the daily papers. To occupy the indolent, column upon column is filled with idle gossip, which can only be procured by intrusion upon the domestic circle. The intensity and complexity of life attendant upon advancing civilization have rendered necessary some retreat from the world, and man, under the refining influence of culture, has become more sensitive to publicity so that solitude and privacy have become more essential to the individual; but modern enterprise and invention have, through invasions upon his privacy, subjected him to mental pain and distress far greater than could be inflicted by mere bodily injury.

The next step in the evolution of our present privacy doctrine as applied to the press came when a young lady in New York, a Miss Roberson, sought an injunction against the use of her picture on flour containers carrying the caption "The Flour of the Family." She had not been asked to sanction this appropriation of her likeness for purely commercial purposes but the New York courts held in 1902 that she had no legal ground for complaint. The New York legislature promptly enacted a bill to confer a right of privacy in such cases as hers and, since its passage, New York and now many other states—some by statute, some by judicial decision—prohibit purely commercial exploitation of anyone's name or picture; i.e. the use of a person's name or picture in connection with a commercial product. The increasingly troublesome problem in New York and elsewhere is the delimitation of the doctrine of privacy beyond such a purely commercial use as was involved in the Roberson case. It is now established that a *fictional* use is also prohibited (unless the person involved is a "public figure" and he is used "incidentally" as background). Recently, however—notably in New York—the doctrine of privacy has been extended to prevent other kinds of uses than these plainly non-informational ones. The right of privacy has been said to prohibit disclosure of "intimate" matters whether involving "public figures" or not. And perhaps even more startling from a civil liberties standpoint are the cases which hold that a right-of-privacy violation is involved when a work about a living person that is not "substantially true" is published.

Thus, in a case brought to court by the great baseball pitcher Warren Spahn in order to enjoin and get damages for the publication of a biography for young adults about him, the intermediate appellate court in New York (in the opinion of many, one of the best courts in the country) said, affirming the injunction (mind you, injunction) and damages awarded by the court below:

It may well be, as defendants urged and, perhaps, proved, that juvenile biography requires the fillip of dramatization, imagined dialogue, manipulated chronologies and fictionalization of events. If so, the publication of juvenile biographies of living persons, even if public figures, may only be effected with the written consent of such persons . . . by writing strictly factual biographies or by confining unauthorized biographies to those of deceased historic persons.

This view was affirmed by New York's highest court, the Court of Appeals. The United States Supreme Court then reversed and sent the case back to the Court of Appeals which on argument adhered to its former position but added a finding that the defendant author and publisher in the Spahn case had proceeded with knowledge that the statements made were false or in reckless disregard of their truth, and that there had been "material and substantial falsifications."

This is a new and dangerous doctrine from a civil liberties standpoint. Such tests of permissible speech and press as "too intimate" or as "substantial truth" would seem to collide with the First Amendment. Those who see in this expanded privacy doctrine a threat to freedom point to its special incongruity in the light of contemporaneous developments in the law of libel. For, in 1964, the United States Supreme Court held for the first time that a civil judgment for money damages in a libel case could be an unconstitutional abridgement of freedom of expression. That decision, handed down in *The New York Times* case, established that public officials may not recover even for false and defamatory statements made about them in their public capacity unless they can prove that actual malice impelled the libels—actual malice meaning with knowledge of the falsity of the statements or such flagrant disregard of their truth as to be tantamount to the same thing. Nothing is simple, and certainly this is so in a democracy when a choice has to be made between two freedoms—privacy in the sense of immunity from press (in its widest sense) exploitation of intimate details or false statements on the one hand, and that "robust, uninhibited" debate which the Supreme Court found in *The Times* case was required by the First Amendment, on the other.

Some elucidation of the real meaning of the right of privacy in this context came from the United States Supreme Court in the spring of 1967 when it reversed the decisions of New York's Court of Appeals in both *The Desperate Hours* case and the Warren Spahn case. The Court appears to have held (and there were many opinions by many justices) that only such privacy violations can be enjoined or punished as are uttered with knowledge of their falsity or in reckless disregard of whether they are true or false. In effect that was an application to the privacy realm of *The New York Times* rule referred to above which held that *public officials* may not successfully sue for libel unless they can show that what is said about them was not only false but also said with knowledge of its falsity or in reckless disregard of its truth or falsity. The full purport of *The Desperate Hours* and Spahn decisions is still to be explored as are two related cases decided even later in the spring of 1967 in the libel area—but with clear implications and direct relevance to the privacy field. These two cases involved Wally Butts and General Walker and raised squarely the question of what is the applicable libel rule to

public figures who are not public officials. Remember that the
Supreme Court had in effect declared *The New York Times*
libel rule applicable to public officials as the applicable privacy test in *The Desperate Hours* and Spahn cases. Hence, it
appears likely that what the Court had to say as to libel of
public figures who are not public officials has considerable
bearing on privacy questions—although exactly what bearing
it is still too early to tell. The four judges who wrote what appears to be the majority opinion in these cases (Chief Justice
Warren joined them in the result they reached, but on different grounds) have come up with a new rule with direct impact on writers and publishers. But its effect on privacy, as
such, is somewhat obscure.

At the time the article which Mr. Butts claimed had libelled
him appeared, he was the athletic director of the University
of Georgia and had overall responsibility for the administration of its athletic program. Georgia is a state university, but
Butts was employed by the Georgia Athletic Association, a
private corporation, rather than by the state itself. Therefore
he was not, in the Court's opinion, a "public official" covered
by *The New York Times* rule and the Court had to decide
what the rule appropriate to public figures as opposed to public officials was. He had won his case in the lower courts and
the decision in his favor was affirmed by the United States
Supreme Court under what is really a "new" rule.

The other case involved a suit by the well-known General
Walker against the Associated Press. General Walker had also
won in the lower court although the Texas Courts did not
hold that he was entitled to the punitive as well as the compensatory damages with which the jury had come in. Both
General Walker (on that issue) and the Associated Press (because he did come out with a large compensatory damage
award) were unhappy with the outcome of the case in the
Texas Courts and the United States Supreme Court agreed to
review it.

The Court passed on both the Butts and Walker cases at
the same time in a decision that will continue to have deep

and far flung influence on all writers and publishers. It sustained the award for Butts against the Curtis Publishing Company and reversed the decisions for General Walker. Why?

One must read the cases many times to ascertain their full significance but its significance is so great in terms of what can be said about public figures that it appears worthy of inclusion here.

The Court stated that there were strong arguments for the plaintiffs' positions in both cases and then went on to say that

> the modern history of the guarantee of freedom of speech and press mainly has been one of a search for the outer limits of that right.

> . . . it is significant that the guarantee of freedom of speech and press falls between the religious guarantees and the guarantee of the right to petition for redress of grievances in the text of the First Amendment, the principles of which are carried to the State by the Fourteenth Amendment. It partakes of the nature of both, for it is as much a guarantee to individuals of their personal right to make their thoughts public and put them before the community (see Holt "Of the Liberty of the Press" in Nelson "Freedom of the Press from Hamilton to the Warren Court" 18–19) as it is a social necessity required for the "maintenance of our political system and an open society." *Time, Inc.* v. *Hill*, supra, at 389. It is because of the personal nature of this right that we have rejected all manner of prior restraint on publication. . . .

The four-man plurality of the Court found that both Butts and Walker were "public figures" in which the public has a legitimate interest but it did not consider that for that reason *The New York Times* rule applied to them. Instead they declared a new rule as a result of the application of which Mr. Butts won his case and General Walker lost his. Basically, the new rule, apparently now applicable to public figures who bring libel suits and certainly bound to have some effect on privacy cases, is concerned with whether the defendant evidenced in the publication complained of "a departure from the kind of care society may expect from a reasonable man performing such activity . . . ." The Court then went on to "hold that a 'public figure' who is not a public official may also recover damages for a defamatory falsehood whose substance makes substantial danger to reputation apparent, on a showing of highly unreasonable conduct constituting an extreme departure from the standards of investigation and reporting ordinarily adhered to by responsible publishers."

In affirming the Butts decision, the Court adverted to the type of criteria it considered relevant under this new test.

The evidence showed that the Butts story was in no sense "hot news" and the editors of the magazine recognized the need for a thorough investigation of the serious charges. Elementary precautions were, nevertheless, ignored. . . . [N]otes were not even viewed by any of the magazine's personnel prior to publication. John Carmichael, who was supposed to have been with Burnett when the phone call was overheard, was not interviewed. No attempt was made to screen the films of the game to see if Burnett's information was accurate, and no attempt was made to find out whether Alabama had adjusted its plans after the alleged divulgence of information.

The Post writer assigned to the story was not a football expert and no attempt was made to check the story with someone knowledgeable in the sport. At the trial such experts indicated that the information in the Burnett notes was either such that it would be evident to any opposing coach from game films regularly exchanged or valueless. Those assisting the Post writer in his investigation were already deeply invoved in another libel action, based on a different article, brought against Curtis Publishing Co. by the Alabama coach and unlikely to be the source of a complete and objective investigation. The Saturday Evening Post was anxious to change its image by instituting a policy of "sophisticated muckraking," and the pressure to produce a successful exposé might have induced a stretching of standards. In short, the evidence is ample to support a finding of highly unreasonable conduct constituting an extreme departure from the standards of investigation and reporting ordinarily adhered to by responsible publishers.

Equally probative of the new test is what the Court had to say in reversing the compensatory damage judgment in General Walker's favor:

In contrast to the *Butts* article, the dispatch which concerns us in *Walker* was news which required immediate dissemination. The Associated Press received the information from a correspondent who was present at the scene of the events and gave every indication of being trustworthy and competent. His dispatches in this instance, with one minor exception, were internally consistent and would not have seemed unreasonable to one familiar with General Walker's prior publicized statements on the underlying controversy. Considering the necessity for rapid dissemination, nothing in this series of events gives the slightest hint of a severe departure from accepted publishing standards. We therefore conclude that General Walker should not be entitled to damages from the Associated Press.

Furthermore, the Court held in the Butts case that the same constitutional standards of misconduct are applicable to compensatory and punitive damages.

Where a publisher's departure from standards of press responsibility is severe enough to strip from him the constitutional protection our decision acknowledges, we think it entirely proper for the state to act not only for the protection of the individual injured but to safeguard all those similarly situated against like abuse. Moreover, punitive damages require a finding of "ill will" under general libel law and it is not unjust that a publisher be forced to pay for the "venting of his spleen" in a manner which does not meet even the minimum standards required for constitutional protection. Especially in those cases where circumstances outside the publication itself reduce its impact sufficiently to make a compensatory imposition an inordinately light burden, punitive damages serve a wholly legitimate purpose in the protection of individual reputation.

The Justices split quite a bit among themselves on various aspects of these cases. Chief Justice Warren's concurring (with the majority) opinion also laid stress on the standard of care which these cases appear to impose on those who disseminate speech and press.

The slipshod and sketchy investigatory techniques employed to check the veracity of the source and the inferences to be drawn from the few facts believed to be true are detailed at length in the opinion of Mr. Justice Harlan [the majority opinion summarized above]. Suffice it to say that little investigative effort was expended initially and no additional inquiries were made even after the editors were notified by respondent and his daughter that the account to be published was absolutely untrue. Instead, the Saturday Evening Post proceeded on its reckless course with full knowledge of the harm that would likely result from publication of the article.

Mr. Justices Brennan and White took somewhat different views and Mr. Justices Black and Douglas adhered in both cases to the positions they have consistently taken, namely, that all these rules—*The New York Times* rule, *The Desperate Hours* rule, and now the rule of due care—expounded in these cases are "wholly inadequate to save the press from being destroyed by libel and, by inference, privacy judgments."
As Mr. Justice Black put it:

Here the Court reverses the case of *Associated Press* v. *Walker*, but affirms the judgment of *Curtis Publishing*

*Co.* v. *Butts.* The main reason for this quite contradictory action, so far as I can determine, is that the Court looks at the facts in both cases as though it were a jury and reaches the conclusion that the Saturday Evening Post, in writing about Butts, was so abusive that its article is more of a libel at the constitutional level than is the one by the Associated Press. That seems a strange way to erect a constitutional standard for libel cases. If this precedent is followed, it means that we must in all libel cases hereafter weigh the facts and hold that all papers and magazines guilty of gross writing or reporting are constitutionally liable, while they are not if the quality of the reporting is approved by a majority of us. In the final analysis, what we do in these circumstances is to review the factual questions in cases decided by juries—a review which is a flat violation of the Seventh Amendment.

It strikes me that the Court is getting itself in the same quagmire in the field of libel in which it is now helplessly struggling in the field of obscenity. No one, including this Court, can know what is and what is not constitutionally obscene or libelous under this Court's rulings. Today the Court will not give the First Amendment its natural and obvious meaning by holding that a law which seriously menaces the very life of press freedom violates the First Amendment. In fact, the Court is suggesting various experimental expedients in libel cases, all of which boil down to a determination of how offensive to this Court a particular libel judgment may be, either because of its immense size or because the Court does not like the way an alleged libelee was treated. . . .

I think it is time for this Court to abandon *New York Times* v. *Sullivan* and adopt the rule to the effect that the First Amendment was intended to leave the press free from the harassment of libel judgments.

Well, there we are, folks, at least for the time being and as you can see, there is much that can be—and has been—said on both sides. Until *The New York Times* decision there didn't appear to be any *national* test of what might or might not be considered libelous or in violation of a right of privacy with a few exceptions such as the *Near* v. *Minnesota* rule against enjoining publishers in advance and the freedom of federal officials from libel suits against them pertinent to their official duties The whole thing is, of course, very much in process but those in the field of public communications will have to march to the beat of the United States Supreme Court drum in this field—at least to the extent they can figure it out. And clearly, that Court is trying simultaneously to preserve two values that are often mutually exclusive—on the one hand, freedom of speech and the press, the essential basis of all other freedoms and, on the other hand, the privacy and reputation of individuals in a world where their preservation is increasingly threatened by the facts of the world itself.

Professor Thomas Reid Powell of the Harvard Law School once defined "provocative" in terms of the ability to deal superficially with profound subjects. It is hoped that in that sense the discussion of the privacy issues in this chapter may be provocative. Once we sort out the strands, we may find different names for the different meanings inherent in the concept of privacy—some of which clearly have a constitutional base, some of which may be destructive of other and, in their context, more important constitutional guarantees. The importance of the issues challenges all who believe in civil liberties to refine their concepts and lend their aid to the legislatures and the courts which will have to face squarely and deal with the problems of privacy for decades to come.

The genius of the U.S. Constitution is that it grows and develops with the nation it governs. Thus, with respect to equality of treatment of Negroes in this country—for many decades, until quite recently—the courts, including the United States Supreme Court, had held that the constitutional guarantees were satisfied by "separate but equal facilities." In other words, integration was not constitutionally commanded. But then, in 1954, the Supreme Court reversed itself and said, "In approaching this problem we cannot turn the clock back to 1868 [when the Amendments were passed] . . . or even to 1896 [when the "separate but equal" decision was handed down] . . . we must consider public education in the light of its full development and its present place in American life throughout the nation."

The United States Supreme Court has now, in several aspects, begun to consider the "right of privacy" in the light of what should be its "full development and its present place in American life throughout the nation" today. But the Court has scarcely begun to fill in the specific areas included within the constitutionally protected "zone of privacy." All of us and especially those of us who are concerned with civil liberties must in these years work to help privacy achieve "its full development" in American life throughout the nation. If, in the words of President Kennedy, we "believe in human dignity as the source of national purpose, in human liberty as the source of national action, in the human heart as the source of national compassion and in the human mind as the source of our invention and our ideas" we will be ever mindful of how technology, doctrine, and freedom of expression affect privacy and vice versa, and at the same time, especially in the *press area,* be alert to watch carefully for any development in the privacy field—technical or legal—which threatens to erode or adversely affect our most fundamental constitutional guarantees of speech and press.

Privacy is clearly a many splendored and complicated thing. Hopefully we will be able to preserve it against an expanding technology capable of destroying it entirely. It is to be hoped that the seeds of privacy and related doctrine mentioned in this chapter will develop into a new kind of Bill of Rights for the individual so that 1984 will turn out to be just another year on the calendar and Mr. Orwell will turn out to have been wrong after all.

*—New York City,*
*September, 1967*

# II

# LEGACIES OF THE
# COLD WAR

## by WALTER MILLIS

The impact of the cold war on civil liberties in the United States was not only severe, it was also searching. Other chapters in this book discuss the legal and political problems of civil liberties in particular areas where the guiding principles, at least, are reasonably clear even if their application is not. But the challenge of the cold war is general and fundamental. It goes to the basic principles themselves, forcing upon upholders of civil liberty questions not always clearly answered at the time and some of which remain unanswered today.

Essentially, the defense of civil liberty is the defense of the just rights and freedoms of the individual against the unjust exactions and repressions of the state. That, however, makes the problem of justice—of drawing the just line between the rights of free men and the claims of the state upon them—the problem which ultimately underlies all civil liberties issues. And it is this very basic problem which cold war raises to its most acute and most baffling form.

It is not difficult to see why this must be so. Whatever the form of government may be, the claims of the state upon the individual always rest in the last analysis upon its obligation "to provide," as our Constitution puts it, "for the common defence." It must defend the military security of the community, its laws and institutions, and its "way of life" against external or internal attack. And the individual's rejection of the state's claims upon him as tyrannical and unjust must again, in the final analysis, rest upon the argument that they are excessive and unnecessary to that end.

In times of peace, when the community does not feel itself threatened either from without or from within, this core issue does not arise. In times of major war it is largely swallowed up in the desperate urgency of the crisis; and regimentations and repressions that would seem patently unjust under other circumstances are accepted without question. But in the ensuing cold war, when the immediate military peril has passed but the military, political, and ideological dangers of an uneasy truce remain, this fundamental problem of civil liberties reasserts itself.

What chiefly distinguishes cold war from other forms of international confrontation—and makes the civil liberties problem so difficult—is the special way in which it intermingles ideology with power politics. After 1945 the American people saw themselves as confronted by the Soviet Union, a great military state having political and power interests in direct conflict with their own; the USSR was animated at the same time by an ideology profoundly repugnant to most Americans, which it was aggressively using as an instrument of power. While Soviet military power was seen (rightly or wrongly) as threatening the destruction of our allies and ourselves from without, communist ideology was seen as undermining the state from within, threatening the "violent overthrow" of its social and political institutions, and in the meanwhile attempting to paralyze its military and diplomatic defenses through espionage, sabotage, and subversion. In such a situation, how far could the upholder of civil liberties go in challenging the measures which the state claimed as necessary to an effective defense?

The Constitution and the Bill of Rights were no longer the sure guide they had been assumed to be. Most of the great principles underlying our concepts of civil liberty had been painfully developed out of the experience of the religious wars of the sixteenth and seventeenth centuries—particularly, in our case, out of the wars between Protestant England and the continental Catholic powers. The long struggle between King and Commons may have involved much more than the simple issue of the national defense; but that the national defense was always a prominent factor cannot be doubted. The rival ideologies were then framed in terms of religious, rather than political, belief; but it is clear that they were dominant elements in the power politics of the time, much as are the conflicts between Buddhists, Catholics, and Muslims in Southeast Asia today. Matters of association and belief were of critical political importance. Heresy and its possible consequences were not merely questions of entertaining "unpopular opinions" but represented a real danger to the state. If some may still doubt whether there was a real Communist conspiracy by Fuchs, Gold, and the Rosenbergs to steal atomic secrets, there is no doubt that there was a real Catholic conspiracy under Guy Fawkes, motivated by faith and belief, to blow up the Protestant king and Parliament. When Jesuit missionaries were hounded through England it was not because of the "errors" of their teaching (subject under Jeffersonian principles to rebuttal in the market place of ideas), but because they were thought to be agents of a foreign power, whose clandestine activities were not to be controlled by logical appeals to reason and argument.

It was only as the ideological struggles gradually lost their importance in international power politics that the devices which are essential to the waging of ideological war—the war of beliefs, of heresies, and of convictions—were also laid aside. Their inefficiency, no less than their injustice, were slowly recognized. The liberties enshrined in our state and Federal constitutions at the end of the eighteenth century declared that such claims by the state over its free citizens were no longer just, necessary, or allowable. Military regimentation and oppression were to be ended, if not by abolishing the "standing army" at least by reducing it to a closely controlled minimum. The individual was guaranteed freedom of speech and assembly and freedom of religious belief; he was guaranteed against self-incrimination and the oath ex officio; he was guaranteed against unwarranted searches and seizures; he was guaranteed the right to jury trial upon indictment only; and so on, as well as being assured in his basic right to representative government. He was protected against all the measures which government had always found most necessary to defense in ideological war. From this point of view the protections were so many declarations that in the affairs of the enlightened eighteenth century state ideological war no longer had any significant place. These great guarantees and protections are the foundation of all our present concepts of civil liberty. Unfortunately, in denying the significance of ideological war to power politics, they could not permanently eliminate it. Whenever it would reappear the foundations of civil liberty were bound to strain, if not to crack.

This was to happen sooner than the authors of the Constitution seem to have expected. The first great civil liberties issue in our history arose within ten years of the ratification of the Constitution, with the adoption of the Alien and Sedition Acts of 1798. The situation, if less extreme, was in some ways not unlike that with which the Soviet Union confronted us a century later. Revolutionary France was a great military power employing a radical ideology as a political and infiltrative weapon in power politics. The international struggle between France and Britain became involved in our own developing party politics. Some French spokesmen claimed that in Jefferson's Democratic-Republicans they had a fifth column in the United States; and it was a claim which the Federalist newspapers and politicians took up with remarkable savagery.

Much as our modern Republicans after 1945 tried to pin upon the Democrats the charge of being "soft on communism," the Federalists labeled the Jeffersonians as the "French party," which if successful could even threaten the overthrow of the government through a "military despotism under foreign influence." They were "disorganizers" (today they would be called "infiltrators") and President Adams went so far as to say that while domestic differences of opinion were "generally harmless, often salutary," when "foreign nations interfere and by their arts and agents excite, and ferment them into parties and factions, such interference and influence must be resisted and exterminated."[1]

This is ideological war. In it one encounters most of the arguments and accusations repeated in the cold war against communism, and the Alien and Sedition Acts of 1798 accurately foreshadowed most of the later assaults on civil liberty. The naturalization of aliens was made more difficult; the President was authorized to arrest or deport any alien whom he considered dangerous to the country, and the Sedition Law made it a crime to publish any false, scandalous, and malicious libel against the government, to stir up sedition or opposition to any lawful act of the President or Congress, or to aid the designs of any foreign power against the United States. The prosecutions and suppressions under the Acts failed, however, in their apparent purpose of defeating Jefferson's election in 1800; on the contrary, the reaction against them was largely responsible for the ultimate destruction of federalism. Jefferson allowed the Acts to lapse, and the episode has since been considered as defining the basic constitutional liberties of speech and belief in the United States. But definition is always subject to interpretation. Should another period arise when matters of speech, belief, loyalty, and allegiance again appear to imperil the state, the definition would clearly be subject to strain.

Civil liberties were unquestionably strained during the Civil

[1] James Morton Smith, *Freedom's Fetters* (Cornell University Press, 1956), p. 17.

War. But there was no cold war afterward, involving a major foreign power, to freeze the war measures into the pattern of peace-time life. Not until our entry into World War I did a massive war effort again raise fundamental questions about the rights and liberties of the individual as against the state's claims in the interests of national defense. Initially, these issues revolved around compulsory military service. The American Civil Liberties Union, founded at this time, grew out of an effort to assert the rights of individual conscience and conviction against the state's claimed right to draft men to combat. The conscientious objector may have asked exemption from killing only as an act of grace from the state; but the implications of his position unavoidably went much deeper than that. Then (as in the Vietnam crisis today) his challenge merged with that of those who opposed the state's right to draft men at all, and of those who opposed this particular war, which could not be waged without compulsory service. The conscientious objector seemed to stand at the forefront of a heresy which could endanger the war effort if not the foundations of the state itself. The Espionage Act of 1918—in effect our second Federal sedition statute—was adopted to deal with it. It made it a crime to "obstruct the draft" or interfere with the war effort by word or deed, which in practice made it a crime to openly oppose the war; and Eugene Debs (with many others) went to prison on what was essentially a charge of sedition.

The fighting ended in November, 1918, but legally the war (and with it much of the war-time legislation) went on for years, while a kind of cold war—the first war on communism—ensued to keep alive the real or imagined perils of treason and sedition. While the states passed a rash of sedition acts and while New York tried to expel its Socialist assemblymen from the legislature, the Federal Government mounted its notorious roundings up and deportations of alien "Red" heretics, by applying, though with much greater severity, the concepts underlying the Alien Acts of 1798. In its formative years the ACLU found no lack of employment for its energies.

In 1919 and 1920, however, the communist ideological peril was not backed by a formidable military power; Russia had been reduced to a shattered chaos and the Bolshevik hopes of world revolution were patently fading. The "little cold war" died out. The reaction in the United States was not unlike that which followed the Alien and Sedition Acts. President Harding commuted Debs' sentence in 1921. The New York Socialist assemblymen regained their seats. The state sedition acts remained largely unused. While the courts, of course, continued to wrestle with issues of free speech and due process, they no longer did so in a cold war context, and the trend of Supreme Court decisions was, in general, toward liberalizing the rights of the individual as against the state. When in the spring of 1930 Representative Hamilton Fish, a conservative Republican from New York, secured authorization for a congressional investigation into "Communist propaganda in the United States and particularly in our educational institutions," it probably aroused more amusement than alarm among upholders of civil liberty. Yet it was, or should have been, a reminder that some fairly fundamental issues of civil liberties had gone unanswered.

The Fish Committee accomplished nothing of consequence and was largely forgotten. But it was the prototype of the investigatory committee set up eight years later under Representative Martin Dies of Texas (on his promise that it would complete its work in seven months) which survives to this day as the House Un-American Activities Committee. By 1938, when the Dies Committee was established, ideological warfare was again a serious matter. The Second World War was visibly approaching. The world-wide communist revolutionary movement was now manipulated and sustained, not by the weak and rag-tag Bolshevist state of the 1920's, but by one of the world's major military powers. The local Communist parties were no longer seen as much of a threat to the internal order of the democracies, but there was no doubt that they had become slavish instruments of Russian power politics,

skillfully wielding a hostile ideology to the confusion and disruption of our own. The Nazis and the fascists were at least
attempting, though less successfully, similar ideological infiltrations of democratic policy. All were using "their arts and
agents," as John Adams had put it, to "interfere" both openly
and clandestinely in our affairs. Under such circumstances,
what a man believed, rather than what he did, was of real political importance, however much the upholder of civil liberties might deplore the fact. The private opinions of a crypto-
Communist or crypto-Nazi were considered to be not simply
"unpopular" or "dissenting," but in themselves dangerous to
the state and to the purity of its political processes.

The uses which the American Communists made of their
power in various institutions, such as the labor unions which
they had infiltrated; their outrageous gyrations in Russian
power issues involving first the United Front and then the
Stalin-Nazi Pact; their conduct in the first stages of the war in
Europe could only confirm the feeling that it was their beliefs
and allegiances rather than their acts that made them a
danger to the state. Members of the Communist party were
excluded from federal employment and relief payments, and
in 1940, with the European war then in full career and Russia
and Germany apparently in alliance, Congress adopted our
first explicit alien and sedition law since 1798. The Smith Act,
in addition to providing for the registration of aliens and the
deportation of the seditious among them, made it a criminal
offense to teach and advocate, or to conspire to teach and advocate, or to have membership in a party which taught or advocated the "violent overthrow" of the government.

In terms the Act, like the Dies Committee mandate, was
impartially directed against the Nazi, fascist, and other political heresies, but the Communists were of course the real tar-
get. Obviously, no one thought the Communists had any
chance of organizing the "violent overthrow" of the government, any more than anyone had seriously thought it of the
French a hundred years before. The protection was not
against an actual overthrow of the Constitution; it was against

the heretical belief, the hostile allegiance, which might inspire lesser acts inimical to the state.

Jefferson had thought the Sedition Act of 1798 "palpably" unconstitutional; and many thought the same of the Smith Act. But such issues were swallowed up by the American entry into the war in 1941. Nazi sedition or subversion clearly held no perils after Pearl Harbor. The Soviet Union became our ally, and the cold war with communism was temporarily in abeyance. The Dies Committee became increasingly inactive and Congress allowed it to lapse in 1944, when the war was at its height. After one or two early cases, the Smith Act went unused during the war and for some years thereafter, and the question of its constitutionality was not to be decided until 1951, eleven years after its enactment.

This is not to say that the war itself presented no civil liberties issues, but they were muted under the overwhelming pressure of what seemed to be military necessity. Peacetime conscription, adopted in 1940 for the first time in our history, might have raised issues similar to those advanced against the draft in 1917, but the ACLU acquiesced in it as essential to the national defense. The most flagrant and unforgiveable violation of civil liberties—the mass deportation and internment of 110,000 people of Japanese heritage (70,000 of them native-born citizens) from the West Coast—aroused no great objection from the country. The preservation of military secrecy was obviously imperative; and few people protested the concept of "security risk" that was growing up among the intelligence and counterespionage services, or the system that resulted in the testing of personnel for "loyalty" on the basis of their associations, speech, and beliefs. It was so difficult to detect an actual spy or enemy agent that the only safe course seemed to be to screen out of sensitive positions all who presented any "risk" of becoming one. But the system of security screening was not highly developed during the war, and few knew much about it or realized its implications. In time of all-out war the issues are never clearly seen. It is in the cold war that they begin poignantly to come home.

In March, 1946 the Secretary of the Navy, James Forrestal, saw Winston Churchill as the latter was returning from giving the address at Fulton, Missouri, often regarded as the opening gun from the Western side in the cold war. The two discussed the new situation in terms which might have been used by one of Sir Winston's sixteenth century ancestors in discussing the menace of Catholic Spain.

> He agreed with my analysis that we are dealing not only with Russia as a national entity but with the expanding power of Russia under Peter the Great plus the additional missionary force of a religion. He mentioned the fact that in his own immediate entourage he had had two men to whom they had to give terms of life imprisonment because they had taken blueprints and other secret documents and delivered them in person to the Russians in London. He said these men had no feeling that they were bound by patriotism or duty to their country but felt that they were acting according to the dictates of a much higher moral code." [2]

This was ideological war. The perils it posed were not simply those of "dissent" or even of opinions "of wrong tendency," but of a fundamental political heresy challenging the basic moral values of the society in the interests of a dangerous and destructive power politics. There is no doubt that the overwhelming majority of Secretary Forrestal's countrymen agreed with his and Churchill's analysis; and one should not underrate the agonizing depths of the dilemma into which it plunged those devoted to the support of a political-legal system founded upon the assumption that heresy was no longer of political importance. Writing ten years later, Leo Pfeffer could still see here the "critical civil liberties problem": "To what extent are constitutional principles and precedents developed in the century-and-a-half struggle to preserve liberties of unpopular Americans applicable to Communists and Communist organizations." It was a problem that divided the Su-

[2] Walter Millis, ed., *The Forrestal Diaries* (Viking Press, 1951), p. 144.

preme Court as deeply as it divided less august citizens. Justice Jackson "found Communism so dissimilar to any other movement or ideology in American history as to render all those principles and precedents practically irrelevant." Justices Black and Douglas found domestic communism "not basically different from any other of the feared and hated ideologies in American history" and therefore thought that the old principles were as applicable to Communists as to any other dissenters. In the decade of 1945–1955 the rest of the Court groped for a middle position, as did the politicians and publicists, but without notable consistency; and in 1956 Pfeffer held that "this problem pervades the entire area of political liberties today." [3] After another decade, one cannot feel that it has been wholly solved, although it has become less painful and less acute.

In the earlier years of the cold war the defenses against communist heresy arose rather slowly. The Dies Committee had been allowed to expire in 1944, and when John Rankin of Mississippi, in a surprise move, secured its revival as a standing, or permanent, committee of the House in January 1945, there was little enthusiasm for it among his colleagues. During 1945 and 1946 it continued to preserve the massive files which the Dies Committee had accumulated on Communists, supposed Communist sympathizers, Communist "front" movements, and Communist infiltrations; but it held few hearings and aroused relatively little excitement. Yet events, both at home and abroad, were steadily building up the pressures of cold war, intensifying the fear and hatred of the communist ideology, and exaggerating the new emphasis on loyalty and security—forces which represented the major challenges of cold war to the concepts of civil liberty.

By intensifying the pressures in these first post-war years the revelation of the atomic bomb played an important part. It was not only that the unbelievably appalling nature of the weapon seemed to put military power politics in a wholly new

[3] Leo Pfeffer, *The Liberties of an American* (Beacon Press, 1956), p. 81.

context; it also raised the importance of military secrecy and "security" in peace time to an altogether new level. The "secret" of the supposed atomic monopoly—what to do with it, whether to "give it to the Russians," how to guard it—was a matter of impassioned debate in the months after Hiroshima. It was not a debate in which anyone wanted the intervention of those whose inner allegiance was to Russian Communist power. Meanwhile, the Atomic Energy Act, adopted in the summer of 1946, set up the most rigorous system for absolute secrecy and security "clearance" ever thrown around a military-industrial effort of this magnitude in the nation's history.

The rapid deterioration of Soviet-Western relations on the international stage of course exacerbated the domestic war on communism. When the Soviet Union in quick succession swallowed the Balkan and East European "democracies," utilizing the disciplined local parties commanded by Russian- or Moscow-trained Communists, it could only confirm the concept of American communism, not as a party or "faction" willing to play by the conventional Jeffersonian rules of the free society, but as a conspiracy exploiting all the rules and democratic protections in the service of an ideology dedicated to their destruction. Admittedly, the facts of politics and political organization are never as simple as they seem. The American society had never in fact been as Jeffersonian as it liked to think itself, and the distinction between "party," "faction," "conspiracy," and treason never as clear-cut as was ordinarily assumed, or as strict adherence to the constitutional verities would imply. But by the beginning of 1947 Pfeffer's "critical civil liberties problem" was bewildering. It was made no less so by the Republican victory in the 1946 congressional elections, and the advent of the 80th Congress. The already sufficiently difficult issues of civil liberties in a cold war were now injected with the toxins of party politics.

The Dies Committee in 1938 had been given the rather simple authorization to investigate "(1) the extent, character and objects of un-American propaganda activities in the United States, (2) the diffusion within the United States of subversive and un-American propaganda that is instigated from foreign countries or of a domestic origin and attacks the principle of the form of government as guaranteed by our Constitution, and (3) all other questions in relation thereto that would aid Congress in any necessary remedial legislation." The standing House Un-American Activities Committee, as reconstituted by Mr. Rankin in 1945, retained the same mandate. But when at the beginning of 1947 it passed under Republican control, with J. Parnell Thomas of New Jersey as chairman, the words of the authorization were given a somewhat drastic reinterpretation. The committee announced an eight-point program:

1. To expose and ferret out the Communists and Communist sympathizers in the Federal Government.
2. To spotlight the spectacle of having outright Communists controlling and dominating some of the most vital unions in American labor.
3. To institute a counter-educational program against the subversive propaganda which has been hurled at the American people.
4. Investigation of those groups and movements which are trying to dissipate our atomic bomb knowledge for the benefit of a foreign power.
5. Investigation of Communist influences in Hollywood.
6. Investigation of Communist influences in education.
7. Organization of the research staff so as to furnish reference services to Members of Congress . . .
8. Continued accumulation of files and records to be placed at the disposal of investigative units of the Government and armed services.[4]

The rationale and technique of the anticommunist heresy hunt had been developing for a long time; with this program the structure was complete. The Dies investigation of "un-American activities" became explicitly an investigation of

[4] Robert K. Carr, *The House Un-American Activities Committee* (Cornell University Press, 1952), p. 37–38.

communism; the investigation of communism became an investigation of Communists and "Communist sympathizers"; the object of investigation was now to expose and punish those holding, or suspected of holding, a belief in the dangerous heresy—even those who by their speech or associations might be suspected of having a tendency toward it. The Committee proposed to "expose and ferret out" the rats in the woodwork of the (democratic) administration; to "spotlight" Communists in the union managements; to expose "Communist influence" in Hollywood and in education; to conduct counterpropaganda; to amass dossiers on individuals and organizations for the use of the established investigative services of the armed services and the civil government. That any of these functions were within the constitutional powers of Congress seemed doubtful; there could be no doubt that they were profoundly repugnant to the spirit, if not the letter, of the First and Fifth Amendments. Yet the agonizing difficulty remained. The facts underlying the whole theory of the heresy hunt were undeniable.

A Communist was not simply a dissenter—however much he might protest that he was—or a mere holder of unpopular opinions. American communism did actually have many of the elements of a disciplined and often clandestine conspiracy, owing its primary allegiance to a great and hostile foreign power, against the native institutions and the "American way of life." The Communists did more or less secretly infiltrate labor unions, pressure groups, the mass media, and so on; a small but cohesive Communist minority could and often did use the democratic forms to take command (in the best Leninist tradition) of the policies of much larger groups and sway their influence toward ends of which the majority membership would never have approved. They did form clandestine "cells" within the Federal Government, which, however effective they ever were in practice, at least threatened to distort national policy to other than the accepted national ends. They did infiltrate union managements. Wherever they went they were trouble-makers. And it was the domestic party and its "sympathizers" which provided the best recruiting ground for Soviet Russian espionage nets. In 1947 and 1948, under the terrible shadow of the atom bomb, espionage was given a value altogether disproportionate to its real importance to international affairs or to the national security.

A series of events in 1947 and 1948 could only magnify these concepts of the communist peril. The testimony of Elizabeth Bentley and Whittaker Chambers before the Un-American Activities Committee gave the first tangible indication that there were, or had been, Communist cells in the Federal Government. In Canada, Igor Gouzenko, the defecting Soviet code clerk, revealed the existence of extensive Soviet espionage nets, largely recruited from native Communists or Communist sympathizers, in both Canada and the United States; and when the British scientist, Alan Nunn May, was imprisoned for revealing atomic information, it was shown that the espionage had penetrated at least to the periphery of the most jealously-guarded of all national secrets. At the end of 1948 the Un-American Activities Committee began to develop its sensational case against Alger Hiss, the high government official who had participated in the Yalta Conference and the negotiations establishing the United Nations, as a Communist espionage agent. Few ever stopped to ask what, practically, all this amounted to as far as the protection of the state or the purity of its policies were concerned. For the intertwined perils of subversion, sabotage, and espionage to be apprehended, not simply from communism but from the heretical belief in the communist ideology, seemed to many if not most Americans indisputable.

But the agonizing question of what should be done about it remained. The answer returned by most upholders of civil liberty—that the same constitutional protections of free speech, association, and due process should be thrown around the Communists as around any other "dissenters"—was possibly the correct one, but was unrealistic in the atmosphere of the time. One answer, advanced by Sidney Hook in his book *Heresy, Yes—Conspiracy, No,* was equally unrealistic. Heresy and conspiracy have been historically only two sides of the same medal; in politics they are conceptually inseparable. Another answer, of which Morris Ernst, an active board member of the ACLU, was a leading exponent, was found in the principle of "disclosure." If one should not and could not constitutionally extirpate the heretic, one could force him to "disclose" his beliefs and allegiances, the sources of his acts, his speech, and his financing. The principle was written into some of the subsequent anticommunist legislation; but aside from the fact that it did not work well in practice, it raised baffling issues of theory with which the ACLU itself is still wrestling twenty years later.

The answer actually adopted by government policy makers and popular opinion in the late 1940's and early 1950's was that communism, as a belief, as a teaching, as a plan of action, as a moral ideal, should be extirpated from the American society. That this violated, and was increasingly to violate, almost every principle to which the upholder of civil liberties was dedicated, is now apparent. But since the denials of due process, the suppressions of speech, the resort to the self-incriminatory oath, the invasions of privacy which inevitably resulted were taken under the color of the law and the Constitution, the principles were not easily seen or stated; and as the pressures of fear, hatred, and partisan politics mounted, even their applicability in face of the communist menace became doubtful. Driven by these pressures to demonstrate its own anticommunism, the Truman Administration in 1948 took up the previously almost unused Smith Act of 1940 in order to secure the indictment of the principal leaders of the American Communist party for the crime of conspiring to teach and advocate the violent overthrow of the government. The extraordinary trial went on through most of 1949. With the government exposing at great length the "ill tendencies" of communist teachings and belief, the inadmissible objectives of communism, the clandestine and conspiratorial methods to which it resorted, this was quite plainly a trial of heresy of a sort which most people supposed to be barred under the Constitution. Unfortunately, the violent appeals of the defense attorneys to that document and the excesses of the mobs that gathered in protest outside the court could only support the uneasy doubt as to whether Communists were thus entitled to exploit the liberties guaranteed them by a Constitution they avowedly wished to destroy.

It was an intellectually painful period for the upholders of civil liberty. Was the communist menace in all its forms and aspects sufficient to justify this seemingly gross departure from First Amendment principles? The jury decided that it was; that the teaching and advocacy of communism was equivalent to the teaching and advocacy of "violent" overthrow and therefore a criminal sedition. These Smith Act convictions were crucial to the domestic history of the cold war. If they stood, they would open the way to almost any device for the suppression and extirpation of the communist belief. The anticommunist crusade was pressed rapidly forward. In February, 1950, Senator Joseph R. McCarthy of Wisconsin charged for the first time into this politically inviting field. Whereas the Smith Act had been directed against any seditious teachings, the drastic Internal Security (McCarran) Act of 1950 was directed explicitly against communism. It sought to define "Communist" and "Communist-front" organizations, required them to register and disclose their membership, and imposed heavy disabilities on them, not attached to other conceivably seditious organizations or individuals. The congressional committees redoubled their punitive "investigations." The already vast system of loyalty-security screening in government, in the defense industries, and in many other areas of private employment was pushed to greater and more absurd heights. But a great deal of all this was really predicated on the validity of the Smith Act. If it were held unconstitutional, much else in the war on communism would fall with it. When in 1951 the Supreme Court, under Chief Justice Vinson, in a 6 to 2 decision, finally affirmed the Smith Act convictions, it knocked out the major foundation of the civil liberties position. This decision in the Dennis case was the high point in the impact of the cold war on civil liberty. If the Smith Act was constitutional, by reason of the present or probable dangers it was intended to avert, it became difficult to argue the illegality of many other measures which were, after all, only its logical consequences. In the Dennis case the decisive battle for civil liberties was lost. What remained were years of holding the peripheral actions until, with the diminution of the international cold war pressures, the Warren Court would begin to recognize that the decisions reached in the Dennis Case had been a mistake and would gradually start correcting its worst consequences.

It is important to recognize that by the time Senator McCarthy stepped upon the stage all the major elements of "McCarthyism" had been perfected. He did not invent but merely exploited an institutional and conceptual system already well established and on hand. Rather than trying to trace all the intricacies of the laws, regulations, investigatory procedures, court decisions, and controversies in which it was embodied, it seems preferable to attempt a description of the system itself.

In common acceptance, "communism" by 1950 was no longer a political or economic doctrine; it was a conspiracy (so defined in the Communist Control Act of 1954) directed by a foreign power against the safety, security, and internal order of the United States. The American Communist party was not a political party; it was simply the visible manifestation of this conspiracy. A "Communist" was no longer a citizen; he was no longer even a person, to be judged like others on the basis of his acts, speech, and outward emotions. In fact, he was no more than an abstract generalization, like "a criminal." It is not in itself a crime to be "a criminal"; and it was not in itself a crime to be "a Communist." But just as society has to protect itself against criminals as a class, so it was believed that society had to protect itself against "Communists" as a class.

It was this depersonalization of "the Communist" which was at the root of much of the trouble. Criminals are individually recognizable as such when they commit a crime, and society takes steps to protect itself against them. But, aside from the comparatively rare instances of actual espionage, there was no such thing as "committing communism." Nor could "a Communist" be recognized simply by the fact of party membership; he might be a sympathizer or fellow traveler or a "crypto." Being an abstraction rather than a person, a Communist could be defined only as an agent of the Communist conspiracy. But there was no way to translate this abstraction into terms of the living men and women with whom law and government must deal, except by examination of their inner motives and beliefs, something which are inaccessible to anyone but a psychiatrist. The only recourse was not to examine the individual as a person but to infer his real motives from his associations and speech.

At this point in the evolution of the theory, the Communist had ceased to be a person. He had ceased to be a proveable conspirator. He had become anyone who might, from his utterances, his associations, or even his reading matter, be suspected of belonging to our sympathizing with the conspiracy. More than that, he was anyone who might, because of his background or habits, be enlisted or dragooned into the conspiracy at some future time. At this point he had even ceased to be a Communist; he was now simply a "security risk" who might one day conceivably become one. At law, a man could not be convicted and punished for being either a Communist or a security risk. But the undeniable necessity for keeping unreliable or treasonable personnel from sensitive employment in government and defense industry now combined with the fears and passions of the anticommunist crusade to provide an effective means of punishment for both of these abstractions. They could be brought into public obloquy and denied their means of livelihood.

The congressional committees, the now massive investigatory agencies, and private pressure groups were zealous in exposing "Communists" and "security risks" not only in government and defense industry, but in the motion-picture studios, and in the schools and colleges, with the usual penalty being the immediate loss of one's job and the improbability of getting another. In the name of the national security these people were tried and punished not for what they did, not even for what they were in fact, but for what they were thought to be or what it was supposed they might become.

The abuses of this system of largely extra-legal trial and punishment were inevitable and were not only quick in accumulating but were becoming increasingly grotesque as well. The ancient oath ex officio was freely used to secure convictions for perjury when they could not be obtained for the real "crime" of communism. To plead the Fifth Amendment privilege against self-incrimination was in effect to convict oneself of the charge, and the committees seemed more interested in getting their witnesses to condemn themselves by "taking the Fifth" than in trying the allegations against them. In the innumerable "security" hearings people were found "guilty" on rumor and hearsay, on the testimony of faceless witnesses, on the evidence of secret reports to which they had no access and which they could not rebut. Under the Eisenhower revision (1953) of the Truman security order (dating from 1947) the procedures involving testimony and appeal were improved. But the real problem was less procedural than substantive. In general, the testimony on which an individual was "convicted" was factually correct—as an exhaustive study by Adam Yarmolinsky of some hundred security cases demonstrated [5]—but the question of what he had been convicted of remained. When Ensign Landy was denied a commission in the Naval Reserve because he had continued "closely to associate" with a former Communist—his own mother—the facts were not to be denied but the conclusion was verging upon the absurd.

One must grant that Senator McCarthy made a great, if quite unintended, contribution to the restoration of saner perspectives. In exploiting for his own ends the anticommunist

[5] See Adam Yarmolinsky, *Case Studies in Personal Security* (Bureau of National Affairs, 1955).

crusade he only emphasized the evils latent in it. For some four years he reigned supreme, demonstrating to those who could see the tyrannies implied by this whole approach to the communist problem; but not until the televised Army-McCarthy hearings in 1954 did the lesson come home. This was too much. The pursuit of the communist heresy in our midst had become in itself a heresy against the basic principles of American life. In the tenth year of the international cold war, the cold war at home was raising more perils to the American system than any still to be apprehended from international communism or the Soviet Union. Stalin had died in March 1953. It was too early to see what the consequences would be; but it was apparent that the world was changing. An armistice was at last achieved in Korea. The cold war itself was beginning to lose its ominous intensity; and the perils with which the communist "conspiracy" had actually confronted the state were beginning to be seen in a better perspective.

They had always been grossly exaggerated. The actual damage done by Communist espionage, infiltration, and sedition had been really very slight, while the whole massive anticommunist crusade had had little to do with the detection of such instances as occurred. Its purpose was simply to guard against the possibility that such things *might* happen. Even for that it was a blundering and wasteful instrument; and the Warren Court, beginning with *Parker* v. *Lester* in 1955, began to put narrower limits on the denials of due process, the invasions of individual rights, and the disregard of simple fairness that the state could impose for such a purpose. In June, 1957, the Court, in setting aside a Smith Act conviction, came as near to reversing its Dennis decision of 1951 as it could without actually doing so. The professional anticommunists in Congress and outside it of course screamed that the Court was imperilling the nation. But the general public, with the decline of the cold war and the exposure of the follies as well as the injustices of the anticommunist crusade, paid less and less attention. It was to take many hard battles after 1957 to restore a more balanced concept of the cold war reaching a *detente*. By the late 1950's the task had been pretty well accomplished.[6]

Yet the damage to the old established principles had been great and was not wholly reparable. The anticommunist crusade died down not only because it was unjust, but partially because it ran out of Communists. In other words, it succeeded in its basic aim of extirpating the communist ideology from American life. The American Communist party is allowed to continue an exiguous existence; but to be a Communist, or to be suspected of being one, is to be debarred, like a Catholic in seventeenth century England, from all public and much of private office and employment and to be excluded from many other of the normal rights of citizenship. The security screeners no longer find Communist associations in the backgrounds of job applicants, because a whole generation has been forcibly trained not to have any. The "New Left" of today is just as radical, and doubtless presents just as much (or little) danger of "violent overthrow" as did its parents of the Young Communist League; but in general it is not even cryptocommunist and is uninterested in either Russian or Chinese power politics. In most jurisdictions today, to falsely call a man a "Communist" is an actionable libel. An idea, a doctrine, a political faith has been successfully crushed by methods belonging to the seventeenth century heresy hunt rather than to Jeffersonian democracy. It was done in the name of the safety of the state. Was it necessary to that end? It is hard to believe now that it was, yet countless people still think so and the underlying philosophical issue presented by that conviction has not been wholly analyzed or answered.

At the same time, most of the institutional and conceptual apparatus of the anticommunist crusade remains, ready to be reinvigorated whenever ideological war again seems critical to the national security. Like compulsory military service, compulsory loyalty-security screening on a huge scale seems per-

[6] Walter Millis, *Individual Freedom and the Common Defense* (Fund for the Republic, 1957), p. 52 ff.

manently embedded in American life. Its operations are now largely *pro forma*, and those caught in its toils are accorded most of the rights of due process, but the ACLU is still occasionally called upon to intervene in security cases. Pointless loyalty oaths of one kind or another are still widely exacted as preconditions of employment or for the receipt of government benefits. The House Un-American Activities Committee, though restrained by court decisions from its more flagrant abuses of power, still goes its egregious way. And governmental secrecy and security raise ever higher barriers between the citizen and his knowledge of and control over what is done in his name.

These legacies of the cold war remain with us; but they are of less importance in our lives since the cold war has changed its character—if it has not, indeed, virtually reached its end. Americans are still fully alive to the threats implicit in the power rivalries of the Communist and Western powers, but not many of them are still inclined to see these conflicts in terms of Communist conspiracy and subversion. The policy problems are real and perilous, but the notions of ideological warfare no longer fit the real case, and the methods of ideological warfare, which are the antitheses of civil liberty, no longer seem vital to the survival of the state. Russian or Chinese power still raise great threats before us, but they are not primarily the threats of Communist espionage, subversion, and conspiracy, and cannot be dealt with by the heresy hunts appropriate to ideological war. Civil liberty lost ground in the cold war. Some has been painfully regained; but it is unlikely that we shall ever return completely to the liberties of the past. And if ideological war ever again seems essential to the defense of the state, there will doubtless be a recurrence of the excesses of the 1950's, no matter what the Constitution may say.

# III

# RELIGION, THE STATE, THE INDIVIDUAL

## by ROBERT BIERSTEDT

"Almighty God, we acknowledge our dependence upon Thee, and we beg Thy blessings upon us, our parents, our teachers, and our country. Amen."

This was the prayer—simple, straightforward, and apparently innocuous—that the Board of Regents of the State of New York recommended that the school children of that state recite in their classroom exercises. This was the prayer that the American Civil Liberties Union opposed as a violation of the constitutional principle of the separation of church and state. And this was the prayer that the Supreme Court of the United States declared on June 25, 1962, by a 6 to 1 majority, to be an unconstitutional use of the authority of the state—thus arousing a storm of criticism which has only now begun to subside and which will surely rise again. For the Court and the ACLU alike, the prayer, far from being an example of the free exercise of religion, is in fact a threat to that freedom. How can this be so?

This is not the only question, of course, that invites attention in the area of church-state relations in the United States. Nor is it the only question in which the ACLU has been interested or on which it has exerted its very considerable influence. There are others as well. Mr. Justice Rutledge, in his dissenting opinion in *Everson* v. *Board of Education,* wrote as follows:

> Two great drives are constantly in motion to abridge, in the name of education, the complete division of religion and civil authority which our forefathers made. One is to introduce religious education and observances into the public schools, the other is to obtain public funds for the aid and support of various religious schools.

In what follows we shall be concerned with both of those drives, the one to introduce religion into the public schools —whether in the form of Bible reading, the dissemination of Bibles, school prayer, holiday observances, or released time—and the other to give state aid to sectarian education—whether in the form of direct subsidy or in various kinds of services and supplies. Even these do not exhaust the subject. In all of them, however, the ACLU endeavors to support and strengthen the intent and meaning of the First Amendment to the Constitution of the United States, which says "Congress shall make no law respecting an establishment of religion, or prohibiting the free exercise thereof," provisions that extend to the states as well under the Fourteenth Amendment.

There is authentic genius in this rule. Casuists complain that the no-establishment clause, when strictly interpreted, interferes with the free exercise of religion, that in effect it establishes a religion of secularism or of secular humanism, and that we are prevented by strict construction of our own Constitution from giving full faith and expression to our religious impulses. The ACLU maintains on the contrary that the casuists are wrong, that the clauses mean what they seem to mean, and that only by taking them literally can we guard what may be the most important of all civil liberties, the liberty to worship or not to worship as we please and to answer the ultimate questions of human life and destiny in accordance with our own lights and in independence of the government to which we otherwise give allegiance. No government, however instituted, can answer these ultimate questions and any government that tries to do so is exceeding its earthly authority.

We need one more word in preamble. It was written by the late Mr. Justice Frankfurter when he reminded us that "Preoccupation by our people with the constitutionality, instead of with the wisdom, of legislation or executive action is preoccupation with a false value." It is useful to remember that not everything that is constitutional is necessarily wise, and that not everything that is unconstitutional is on that account unwise. The ACLU, in consequence, agrees with most, but not all, of the decisions of the Supreme Court affecting the First Amendment. Or, to put it differently, in the Union's regard for the separation of church and state the Constitution is always present but not always paramount. The ACLU, in short, is dedicated to the principle of the separation of church and state as one of the most important of civil liberties, in independence of what the courts may have to say about it. Fortunately, the Supreme Court has supported in the majority of instances the views of the members of the Union. Unfortunately, however, controversy in this delicate area still prevails and the work of the ACLU, as one of its distinguished founders, Roger N. Baldwin, often remarks, is never done.

In this chapter, therefore, we shall consider not the constitutional history of decisions affecting the First Amendment, but rather the positions of the ACLU on questions that are relatively current and that have, in times both past and present, agitated the American people.

A nation-wide survey in the early 1960's disclosed that half of the public school systems in the United States indulged in devotional services of one kind or another. The percentages were low in the West (7 per cent) and relatively low in the Middle West (24 per cent) but rose 80 per cent in the East and 95 per cent in the South. Almost all of the schools in the South reported that they were teaching "spiritual values" as distinct from "moral values," and almost two-thirds provided materials to teachers for this purpose. Regular chapel exercises were held in 70 per cent of Southern schools and Bible readings in 75 per cent. Two other practices, released time for religious exercises and bus transportation for parochial school students, were found to be especially common in the East. In that region only an eighth of the schools had regular religious exercises but almost half of them had released time programs and more than a third provided transportation. With respect to actual religious observances, only 15 per cent of the school superintendents in the entire survey felt that they were improper in the schools and almost 90 per cent reported some celebration of Christmas.

There are those, of course, who respond to this situation with equanimity and even satisfaction. Many of these practices continue because it occurs to no one in the local community to object to them, or because of the courage it takes to challenge views adhered to by an overwhelming majority in those communities, or because of the time and money and effort involved in seeking legal redress. Professor Arthur E. Sutherland of the Harvard Law School even sees some merit in these difficulties.

The great multitude of comparatively minor religious manifestations which obtain in many grade and high schools probably thrive on local public approval. Most of them escape official interference because of the sheer inertia of the legal machinery, which tends to discourage prosecution by disgruntled taxpayers and parents, of more than a few cases. No one should welcome judicial delay, expense, and uncertainty. Nevertheless, the difficulties met by citizens who start lawsuits on constitutional ground to enjoin local authorities from conducting some minor religious observances in the public schools may have some good aspects. The practical impossibility of consistent and doctrinaire constitutional literalism in matters of church and state throughout our federal nation may be one of the curious benefits of the system. It seems to be one of those benign paradoxes which permit an adjustment of localism to national policy, and so make life reasonably tolerable in our widespread and diverse nation.[1]

It should be added immediately that this is Professor Sutherland's relaxed view, not the view of the American Civil Liberties Union.

Nevertheless, Professor Sutherland has a point. The point gains weight from the fact that although Protestants may be a minority in many of the larger urban centers, the American culture is still a Protestant culture and operates on Protestant premises. The prominent sociologist, Everett Hughes, once remarked that the culture of French Canada is so Catholic that even the freethinkers are Catholic. One may similarly say that the culture of the United States, in its economic ethic certainly and in most of its norms and ideas, is Protestant.

The impropriety therefore, not to say the unconstitutionality, of reading from the Protestant Bible in the public schools, or the singing of Christian carols at the Christmas season, or giving thanks to a Protestant deity on Thanksgiving, does not occur to the majority of the citizens in their local settings. In the local as opposed to cosmopolitan cultures everyone is religious and everyone is Christian. One is re-

[1] Arthur E. Sutherland, "Public Authority and Religious Education," Nicholas C. Brown, ed., *The Study of Religion in the Public Schools* (American Council on Education, Washington, D.C., 1958), pp. 45–46.

minded of primitive peoples throughout the world who are unable to comprehend the concept of people unlike themselves and who use the same word for themselves that they use for all mankind. One is similarly reminded of the late Warren Austin, former ambassador to the United Nations, who once quite unconsciously illustrated the point by remarking that the Jews and the Arabs should settle their conflicts in accordance with good Christian principles!

In short, we live in a society in which the adjective "Christian" has two synonyms, one of which is "good" and the other is "religious." Anything that is good is both religious and Christian and anything that is religious is both good and Christian. The notions that there may be other religions, that these other religions may also be "good," that unbelievers might conform to the highest of ethical principles, that there may be an incompatibility between religion and morality, that religious freedom requires a prohibition upon saying the Lord's Prayer in the public school would seem quite foreign in the local community. It is only in these terms that we can explain the paradox that the Texas Baptists, for example, are formidable champions of the separation of church and state, and refuse any and all public funds for their own use, and at the same time support in Texas a public school system in which the schools take a religious census of their pupils, in which the public school teachers on Mondays check the attendance of their pupils at Sunday school the day before, and in which many public high schools offer academic credit for courses in religion.

A still more recent survey, conducted by the Associated Press in 1965, indicated that three years after the Supreme Court decision in *Engel* v. *Vitale*, to be discussed below, the ban on prayer continues to be ignored in school district after school district throughout the nation.

The twenty-two-word prayer quoted at the beginning of this chapter was composed by the Board of Regents of the State of New York, which recommended its use in the schools of that state at the opening of the school day. Local school boards were thus encouraged but not required to use it. After several years of inconclusive deliberation the Herricks school district on Long Island decided to try it, and in so doing set in motion a series of events which led ultimately to the Supreme Court. The prayer was designed to express a sentiment to which, it was thought, no one would object, and it was cast in words supposedly as non-denominational as possible. It was nevertheless a prayer, and a number of parents in the district, led by Lawrence Roth, felt that if the State of New York could tell their children what to pray, how to pray, and when to pray, there would very soon be no limits to what the state could do in the sphere of religion. Accordingly, Mr. Roth communicated his concern to the New York Civil Liberties Union, which immediately offered counsel in the person of William J. Butler, a member of its Board of Directors. Four petitioners joined Mr. Roth, out of a much larger number of interested parents, all of them with "standing" in the legal sense, and the five then included two members of the Jewish faith, one Unitarian, one a member of the Ethical Culture Society, and the last an unbeliever. They petitioned the court to enjoin the school board from continuing the practice. They lost their case in several lower courts, on the ground that a simple prayer from which the pupils had a right to excuse themselves does not constitute an establishment of religion; but finally, on April 3, 1962, it reached the Supreme Court of the United States.

The question has arisen as to why the highest court decided to hear the case. There are thousands of cases clamoring for attention and only a small minority can ever come to the highest of judicial decision. As Professor Paul Freund of the Harvard Law School has remarked, the case could easily have been dismissed on the ground that the parents had insufficient interest. Their financial burden as taxpayers was not increased and participation in the prayer was not required although (and this is important from the legal point of view) an affirmative act on the part of a child was necessary in order for him to be excused. The Court, however, follows two maxims among others, one of them *De minimis non curat lex* (the law does not take account of trifles) and the other *Obsta principiis* (resist the beginnings, or beware the entering wedge), and it was the second of these that proved to be controlling. Furthermore, an important question of constitutional law was at issue. The Court therefore heard the case and on Monday, June 25, 1962, handed down its now historic decision supporting the petitioners by a vote of 6 to 1, Mr. Justice Potter Stewart dissenting.

The majority opinion was written by Mr. Justice Black and in it he gave brilliant expression to the principles that motivate the ACLU in its endeavors to defend the last full measure of freedom for the individual citizen who might, in this case, be a lonely child. Justice Black traced the history of religious freedom—or the lack of it—in England and the colonies and concluded that "the constitutional prohibition against laws respecting an establishment of religion must at least mean that in this country it is no part of the business of government to compose official prayers for any group of the American people to recite as part of a religious program carried on by government."

If it is argued, on the other hand, that the Regent's prayer is a fairly inconsequential thing and that the ACLU should conserve its efforts for more important battles, the answer must be that there are no more important battles than one involving the freedom of conscience and the freedom of religion. As Justice Black himself concluded:

To those who may subscribe to the view that because the Regents' official prayer is so brief and general there can be no danger to religious freedom in its governmental establishment, however, it may be appropriate to say in the words of James Madison, the author of the First Amendment:

"It is proper to take alarm at the first experiment on our liberties . . . . Who does not see that the same authority which can establish Christianity, in exclusion of all other religions, may establish with the same ease any particular sect of Christians, in exclusion of all other sects?

"That the same authority which can force a citizen to contribute three pence only of his property for the support of any one establishment, may force him to conform to any other establishment whatsoever."

And so we go back to Madison himself for an affirmation of *Obsta principiis*.

Any prayer, of course, can be offensive to some people and that is what is finally wrong with all prayers in the public schools of a free society. The Lord's Prayer, for example, is used by millions of people in this country, and yet it too is defective in this respect. There is not one version of it but several and each Christian group holds with tenacity to its own. If it were permitted in the public schools all of the following questions would require *political* decisions:

Should the school authority include the words "For thine is the kingdom, and the power, and the glory, for ever," which are omitted in the Roman Catholic version?

Should the children say "Forgive us our trespasses," or use the word "debts" instead, or possibly "sins" or "wrongs"—each of which has support in some versions?

What should be said about the view of some, possibly more religiously dedicated than others, that the supplication "Lead us not into temptation" is blasphemous because no good God would do so, and to assume the contrary, as this expression clearly does, is to speak evil of the deity?

And finally, the most earnest and literal of Christians could object not only to the Lord's Prayer but to all prayers that are spoken in unison for the reason that, on the authority of Jesus himself, prayer is a private affair. Jesus said (Matthew 6:5): "And when ye pray, ye shall not be as the hypocrites; for they love to stand and pray in the synagogues and in the corners of the streets, that they may be seen of men. Verily I say unto you, They have received their reward. But thou, when thou prayest, enter into thine inner chamber, and having shut thy door, pray to thy Father who is in secret, and thy Father who seeth in secret shall recompense thee."

It is not clear, in short, how a teacher, a principal, a superintendent, a school board, a state commissioner of education, a board of regents, a court, or a legislature could resolve questions of this kind. Any attempt to do so would fire the coals of controversy that are now kept quiescent by the damper of the First Amendment.

Needless to say, the ACLU is with the Court in these decisions and the Court, one might say, is with the Union. But whatever the decision regarding the constitutionality of school prayer, whatever the opinion of the Court, the Union would still object to religious exercises in the public schools on the ground that it is impossible to eradicate from them the quality of compulsion. To require immature pupils of many religious faiths or of no religious faith at all to recite in unison a prayer containing sentiments to which some of them—*or only one*—may not subscribe is to offend against the canons of courtesy and of common decency. To do so pins these children on the horns of a serious dilemma, one horn of which is labeled ostracism and the other horn hypocrisy. The child's world is a small one, and the school is a very large part of it. At no other stage of life are the pressures to conform so extreme, so palpable, and so intimately imposed. The child who does not share, for whatever reason, the views of the majority has two equally intolerable alternatives—either to remain silent at prayer time and thus invite the contempt of his comrades, or to say the words with the others and thus do violence to his own conscience. The ACLU believes that this choice should not be within the power of the state to demand.

The decision in *Engel* v. *Vitale* aroused, as might have been expected, a storm of protest, almost all of it missing the point. A Republican congressman, Frank J. Becker of New York, called it "the most tragic decision in the history of the United States." Cardinal Spellman was "shocked" and "frightened."

Senator Herman Talmadge of Georgia declared that a blow had been dealt to all believers in a supreme being. Bishop James A. Pike, himself often accused of apostasy, felt that the Court "had deconsecrated the nation." But it was left to a congressman from Alabama, George W. Andrews, to utter the most reprehensible words when he complained that the Court had first put the Negroes in the schools and had then put God out. A number of other congressmen introduced vociferous objections into the *Congressional Record* and none defended the decision. It remained for President John F. Kennedy, himself always vulnerable on religious issues, to say with calm and assurance that the best remedy was for American citizens to pray more at home and in church and thus "to make the true meaning of prayer much more important to the lives of all our children." The governors of the several states, however, in convention at Hershey, Pennsylvania, in the summer of 1962, almost unanimously called for a constitutional amendment to restore the right to pray in the public schools.

A proposed amendment was not long in coming. It was offered and named after Frank J. Becker, quoted above, and a major drive to introduce it was made in the late spring of 1964. More than two hundred constitutional lawyers—professors of law and law school deans—formally opposed the amendment and any other proposals designed to permit religious exercises in the public schools and made the important point that "If the first clause of the Bill of Rights, forbidding laws respecting an establishment of religion, should prove so easily susceptible to impairment by amendment, none of the succeeding clauses will be secure."

The position of the ACLU in opposition to the Becker amendment was presented by a member of the Board of Directors, the Reverend Edward O. Miller, Rector of St. George's Episcopal Church in New York City. He asked if religion in the United States was so weak that it needed the support of the government; asked whether the great American experiment of freedom of religious belief had been a failure; spoke his doubts (and those of other members of the religious community) about turning against our historic tradition and adopting an official or civic religion; pointed to the dangers of divisive sectarianism (Shall we have Catholic prayers in metropolitan Boston, Protestant prayers in Atlanta, Mormon prayers in Salt Lake City, and Muslim prayers in Harlem?); asked whether compulsory prayer in the classroom could ever be consonant with the *free* exercise of religion; suggested that majority rule in affairs of religion would impair the equality of citizens whose faith was different; declared that coercive prayer served neither God nor religion; and concluded that "The threat is not the secularization of our schools but the secularization of our religion."

After the initial shock of the prayer decision, attributable in part at least to inaccurate reporting in the press, many religious leaders of different faiths came publicly to support this point of view and recognized the dangers to religion in an abrogation of the First Amendment. The Reverend Dr. C. Emanuel Carlson, for example, Director of the Baptist Joint Committee on Public Affairs, said:

> Twenty million Baptists in all parts of our land appreciate the part that the Supreme Court has played in protecting our freedom of religion. Anyone who stops to think through the meaning of prayer, and to find it in the relationship of a person to his God, will automatically conclude that this is something that lies beyond the scope of government.

And Senator Philip A. Hart (Democrat, Michigan) observed:

> I'm a Catholic and I hope a devout one, but I think that the public school classroom is no place for me to try and impose my word formula for prayers on children who don't share it, and for that very reason, I don't want my children in a public school classroom to be exposed to some one else's religion or formula; so that I think the

Supreme Court decision was right and proper.

And that, of course, is precisely the point, the point that the ACLU would hope that all citizens in this free society would come to appreciate.

After the prayer decision, the problem of Bible reading in the schools requires only a brief note because the issue, in essence, is the same. Two cases, one concerning Abingdon Township, Pennsylvania, and the other the public schools of Baltimore, have been decided in a manner consistent with *Engle* v. *Vitale*. Now the question was not whose prayer but whose Bible. And why the Bible, the sacred book of one religion, rather than the sacred book of some other religion?

In the 1830's, before the first waves of Catholic immigration, the King James version of the Bible was a common sight in the public schools and reading from it as a form of religious instruction a common practice. The new Catholic immigrants, however, began to insist that the Douay version was the only true Bible and bitter strife ensued, resulting in the expulsion of a hundred Catholic children from a single school in Boston because they refused to indulge in the Biblical exercises and in the same city in the flogging of a Catholic child for refusing to read the Protestant Bible. The depth of emotion engendered can be gauged by the formation of an American and Foreign Christian Union which maintained that the King James version would remain in the classroom, in spite of Catholic protests, "so long as a piece of Plymouth Rock remains big enough to make a gun flint out of." Riots broke out in New York and Philadelphia and in the latter city two Catholic churches and several Catholic schools were burned. In our own times a school board in California voted to institute Bible reading in the schools and then hastily rescinded it when the Catholic bishop of the area demanded that the Douay version be used. The use of the schools for Bible distribution, as has been attempted by the Gideon Society, whether free or at a price, and even when acceptance is wholly voluntary, is also opposed by the ACLU.

The case for keeping the Bible out of the public schools is clear enough when one recognizes that three major religious groups in the United States—Protestants, Catholics, and Jews—use considerably different versions of it, that two other significant religious groups—the Church of Latter Day Saints and The Church of Christ, Scientist—have books of their own, *The Book of Mormon* and *Science and Health with Key to the Scriptures*, and that the Black Muslims, a majority in some localities in South Chicago and Harlem, adhere to the *Koran*. The reading of the sacred texts of any religion would resurrect the old post-Reformation doctrine of *cuius regio, eius religio* (whose religion, his religion), in which the peasants of Germany had to conform to the religion, whether Protestant or Catholic (and frequently changing), of the prince of the territory in question and thus instituting a territorial test of religious truth. It is this sort of thing, of course, which the First Amendment was designed to prevent.

To say that religious exercises, in the form of prayer and Bible reading, should be excluded from the public schools does not mean that the schools may not teach *about* religion. There is in fact an enormous difference between teaching religion, in the sense of exercising it, and teaching about religion, in the sense of the dissemination of knowledge. In the latter case the children can be taught the sacred books of the various world religions as contributions to the world's literature. The importance of religion in society is so great that children ought perhaps to learn—and where better than in the public school—that there are many religions in the world, almost as many as there are separate societies, and that they all have their sacred books and their sacred ceremonies.

To learn something about these books and ceremonies helps to free the children from the provincialisms of time and place and circumstance and to lead them out into worlds as yet unknown—which is, in essence, the purpose of education. It is useful, for example, for the American Protestant or Catholic child to know that even before the rise of Christianity a wise man in Greece, whose name was Socrates, composed a prayer that contains a moral lesson for those who live in any period of the world's history: "Beloved Pan, and all ye other gods who haunt this place: give me beauty of the inner soul, and may the outward and the inner man be at one." And it is similarly useful for the American Jewish child to learn of a medieval Italian monk, Saint Francis of Assisi, who prayed: "Lord! Make me an instrument of Thy peace. Where there is hatred, let me sow love; where there is injury, pardon; where there is doubt, faith; where there is despair, hope; where there is darkness, light; and where there is sadness, joy." One concludes, therefore, that the knowledge of religion is one thing, its practice quite another. The ACLU believes that it is necessary to sustain the distinction.

The question of the observance of religious holidays affects both the public school and the larger community. Here again the Union endeavors to maintain the distinction just mentioned. In a society that is predominately Christian, and in which therefore the Christian holidays of Christmas and Easter play so large a part, it is not unreasonable to suppose that the symbols of these holidays should find their way into the schools. Thus, there are the traditional Christmas carols, an old and treasured part of the Christian heritage and a part, too, of the general cultural heritage of those nations in which Christianity has flourished. The Christmas tree and the crèche are similar symbols, although the former far antedates Christianity as a survival of older pagan festivals celebrating the winter solstice. Shall these songs, ceremonies, and symbols, too, be prohibited in the public schools?

To this question the Union has responded with a reaffirmation of the principle of the separation of church and state. There is no objection to explaining the meaning of various religious practices and observances—whether Christmas, Chanukah, Ramadan, or whatever—because these are items of knowledge. But observance of any of them as an expression of orthodoxy ought rigorously to be forbidden, even in those communities that are wholly homogeneous in their religious faith. There is the additional proviso that no student should be compelled to participate even in such an apparently innocuous exercise as carol singing if it offends his conscience to do so. Ideally, therefore, no religious symbol should ever appear in a public school, even if it offends no one; but if Christmas, for example, can be the occasion of a two-week vacation from school, it seems unrealistic to make no mention of it. The answer here is to act with such wisdom and restraint that the children will neither be exposed to religious persuasion nor be deprived of knowledge.

With respect to community observance of religious holidays—the exhibition of a crèche on the court house lawn or, as in Boston, the expenditure of public funds for elaborate Christmas displays on the Boston Common—these are ubiquitous but nevertheless unconstitutional. Here the Union relies upon the decision reached in the Everson case that "No tax in any amount, large or small, can be levied to support any religious activities or institutions, whatever they may be called, or whatever form they may adopt to teach or practice religion." The impropriety—to say nothing of the illegality—of taxing Jewish and freethinking citizens for the sake of Christian religious exhibitions is clear.

A brief word may be said also about the baccalaureate service. It is customary in Protestant communities throughout the nation to schedule such a service in a local church on the Sunday preceding the commencement exercises. The graduating class attends in a body, garbed in academic dress, and listens to a sermon preached by a local minister. So long as the community, and the graduating class, was entirely Protestant, no one thought of entertaining an objection. In recent years, however, Catholic bishops have begun to express their objections and have prohibited Catholic students from attending. The Union here supports the bishops on the grounds, as a former Executive Director of the Union, Patrick Murphy Malin, said: It is "unlawful and unconstitutional for the public authority to introduce elements of religious worship into any public exercise, even if attendance is completely voluntary," and, even further, that "constitutional prohibition operates even in the absence of a single objection."

The separation of church and state in this country has consequently led to a certain dissatisfaction among all organized religious groups with the amount of religious instruction their children receive. The school day, from morning to midafternoon, and the school week, from Monday through Friday, occupies the dominant proportion of the children's time, as it does of their attention, and there is little left for religious instruction. There is, of course, the Sunday school, for one hour preceding church services on Sunday; but this seems, by its very brevity, to offer a poor contrast to the public school. As a result, many of the churches have endeavored in various ways to compensate for what seems to them a disprivileged position. Thus, there are efforts to have after-class schools, Saturday schools, and Daily Vacation Bible Schools during the summer months, in which the children would receive their religious education.

Efforts to enlarge these activities have involved the public schools and have taken various forms. In one community, Champaign, Illinois, religious instructors representing the various faiths entered the schools once a week during the regular hours and conducted religious classes for one-half hour, the children going to different rooms for this purpose. This practice was challenged by the mother of one of the pupils, Mrs. Vashti McCollum, and when the case came to the Supreme Court the justices, with one dissent, held that it was unconstitutional. Mr. Justice Black, speaking for the majority, said that "Here not only are the state's tax-supported public school buildings used for the dissemination of religious doctrines. The State also affords sectarian groups an invaluable aid in that it helps to provide pupils for their religious classes through use of the state's compulsory public school machinery. This is not separation of Church and State."

If religious instruction in the public school building, even when offered without cost to the school board, is unconstitutional, the alternative was to release the children to religious classes outside of the building. This was the case in New York City, where the pupils went to religious centers for religious instruction, on written request of their parents, leaving behind those who did not present such requests. In addition, the churches cooperating in the program sent back to the school the names of the children who had been released but who did not appear for their religious lessons. When this practice was challenged the Court upheld it by a vote of 6 to 3 in the case known as *Zorach* v. *Clauson*.

Like many social policies, however, this one had certain unanticipated consequences. The first of these is that academic credit appears to be given for religious instruction on released time in an increasing number of school districts. A second concerns the time at which pupils are to be released. In a school district in Rhode Island, for example, where 80 per cent of the students were Catholic, the program began with a released hour once a week at the end of the school day. The Catholic authorities contended, however, that students were more alert at the beginning of the day, and so the change was made over the protests of both Protestant and Jewish religious leaders. A third concerns the fate of those students who do not request release. Where the program is most successful and involves the largest number of students, the few who remain in their classrooms receive no continuous instruction and have little to do but twiddle their thumbs. In the opinion of the ACLU the only solution that would escape constitutional defect would be to release all of the children at the same time every week, to do what they or their parents will, thus turning the program into one of dismissed rather than released time. The Union, in short, continues to agree with the Court minority in the Zorach case on the ground, expressed by Mr. Justice Black, that under released time programs the state "makes sects beneficiaries of its power to compel children to attend secular schools."

In recent years a different device has come to public attention. It is called shared time or dual enrollment and is in operation in some districts and in some form in more than twenty states. Under this plan the education of public and parochial school children is shared by the two kinds of schools, the children spending part of the day in one kind of school and part of the day in the other. Thus, parochial school children attend the public school for instruction in such secular subjects as typing, gymnastics, physical education, foreign languages, mathematics, physics, chemistry, industrial arts, grammar, and English composition. They attend the parochial school, on the other hand, for instruction in disciplines that exhibit or require religious differences in treatment, such as literature, history, social studies, and, of course, religion itself.

In one respect shared time raises all of the issues, constitutional and otherwise, that are involved in the released time programs. In another respect, however, shared time stands in contradictory opposition to released time. In the latter, the children are released from the public school for parochial instruction. In the former, parochial school students are released from the parochial school for secular instruction. From still another point of view, shared time raises not only all of the problems associated with released time but in addition the equally serious question of public financial aid to parochial education and, therefore, of government support of religion.

Opinions on shared time cover a wide spectrum. Like many other questions, this is one that has been debated in terms of both constitutionality and social policy. With respect to constitutionality, for example, at least three points of view have been presented and defended: (1) that shared time is forbidden by the Constitution; (2) that it is permitted by the Constitution; and (3) that it is required by the Constitution. With respect to social policy, the arguments are similarly diverse, ranging all the way from the contention that shared time is in the best interest of all of the children to the view that it is only an ill-concealed attempt to aid parochial schools in their struggle to survive and grow.

The arguments in favor of shared time include the view that by this device parents of parochial school students are not wholly deprived of the benefits of the taxes they pay to support the public schools; that by doing this we have found a solution to a perennial problem, that of federal aid to parochial schools, and which would no longer be needed or desired; that the program represents a decent compromise in that parochial school children on the one hand are not denied certain public benefits available to other children nor on the other hand are public monies spent for religious education; that the program can probably win constitutional sanction; that it will broaden support for public schools in that parents of parochial school students will take an interest in them and will vote for bond issues that they now vote against; that children in both kinds of schools will have a broader experience and thus a better education; that under shared time the pressure for religious exercises in the public schools will disappear; and that shared time will reduce the divisiveness in American life that otherwise occurs when the children go off to separate schools.

Unfortunately, however, as Thomas Hobbes once observed, to every argument one equally good can be opposed. The arguments against shared time include the view that the divisiveness supposed to be cured will in fact persist and become even more visible if parochial school children are moved in groups and placed in classrooms as distinguishable visitors, and especially if they wear distinctive dress; that the administrative problems are insuperable, especially in the utilization of space and in the arrangement of schedules; that the cooperative planning required on the part of parochial and public authorities would raise a constitutional doubt; that, from the parochial and especially Catholic point of view, it would violate the concept of education as a seamless web of which religion is an integral part; that it would lead to the destruction of the public school system as we know it and encourage the proliferation of private schools, including private *political* schools; that it would continue church-state conflicts on another and even more regrettable level, namely in the schools themselves; and that it would expand the influence of organized religion upon the public schools.

These arguments, both pro and con, have different degrees of merit and are listed in no particular order of significance. One of the arguments in support of the constitutionality of the program is that since the public schools are obligated to accept all of the children all of the time, there is no clear reason why they cannot accept half of the children half of the time—although the proportions, of course, would vary in different communities. Certainly, in other terms, there could be no objection to a Catholic child spending two of his four high school years in the parochial school and the other two in the public school, and if this is possible successively it is hard to argue that it is not possible concurrently. Similarly, if it is said that shared time would be of substantial benefit to the parochial schools, and therefore an aid to religion, it can be answered that the very existence of the public school system is in the same sense an aid to religion, since without it the various denominations would have to assume the burden of education for themselves—as in fact they did in colonial times. Finally, the argument that shared time would result in extra cost to the public school system is without constitutional merit in view of the fact that if all the parochial schools in the country were to close today the children who attend them would have a perfect right to enroll in the public schools tomorrow.

It seems possible to conclude, therefore, although the ACLU has not adopted this position, that shared time programs do not violate the principle of church-state separation providing that they are administered solely under the public authority and providing that certain safeguards are consistently and rigidly observed. Among these safeguards are the requirements that no decisions whatever—with respect to textbooks, teachers, curricula, schedules, school sites, and so on—be made by private school officials; that the program serve public rather than parochial objectives; and that none of the benefits be given to parochial schools themselves but only to parochial school students when in actual attendance in the public schools. Whether or not these prohibitions would be observed in actual practice, of course, continues to be a serious question and one that will help to determine ACLU opinion on the matter.

On federal aid to education as such the ACLU has no position. It is not a civil liberties issue but rather one of social, political, and educational policy. On federal aid to religious education, however, on aid to parochial schools, on aid to anything but the public schools, the position of the Union is clear, consistent, and concise. It conforms to the powerfully stated views of Mr. Justice Black in *Everson* v. *Board of Education*:

> The "establishment of religion" clause of the First Amendment means at least this: Neither a state nor the Federal Government can set up a church. Neither can pass laws which aid one religion, aid all religions, or prefer one religion over another. Neither can force nor influence a person to go to or to remain away from church against his will or force him to profess a belief or disbelief in any religion. No person can be punished for entertaining or professing religious beliefs or disbeliefs, for church attendance or non-attendance. No tax in any amount, large or small, can be levied to support any religious activities or institutions, whatever they may be called, or whatever form they may adopt to teach or practice religion. Neither a state nor the Federal Government can, openly or secretly, participate in the affairs of any religious organizations or groups and vice versa. In the words of Jefferson, the clause against establishment of religion by law was intended to erect "a wall of separation between Church and State."

No aid, in short, means no aid, and any transgression, direct or indirect, would violate the establishment clause of the First

Amendment. All of the states except Vermont and Rhode Island, incidentally, have similar provisions in their own constitutions and have been required to have them since 1876 in order to qualify for admission into the Federal Union. On the other hand, any religious group has the constitutionally respected right to operate and maintain its own schools at its own expense provided that the educational program conforms to standards set by the state.

What is clear in theory, however, is not necessarily clear in practice. No public money may be given to a parochial school. But suppose the money is given to the child rather than to the school? What then? In other words, there has developed a theory of "child benefit" according to which it is the child and not the school (or the religious sect) that is the beneficiary of the expenditure. According to this reasoning, it is proper that the state pay for transporting the children to and from the parochial school, to purchase textbooks for the children's use, and to provide for school lunches and medical and dental examinations. To this contention the ACLU responds that there is nothing improper in state contributions to the physical welfare of the child, as to that of all the citizens, and would thus see no objection to the medical and dental examinations, to the school lunches, or, for that matter, to police and fire protection at the parochial school. None of these concerns either education or religion. The textbooks are in a different category because they would be chosen by parochial school authorities to coincide with and to promote their own sectarian beliefs. The transportation controversy was decided, of course, in *Everson* v. *Board of Education,* in which the Court approved of the bus subsidy by a 5 to 4 vote. The ACLU continues to dissent, however, as do several of the states, and continues to regard the transportation of parochial school pupils as an aid to religion, just as public payment for custodial and janitorial services in the parochial schools would be. The argument in terms of child benefit could justify state support of all parochial education on the ground that education itself is a benefit to the child. For this reason the Union believes that the child benefit theory is not only "unsound and devious, but is extremely dangerous."

Recent legislative efforts to combat poverty and improve the educational opportunities of deprived children have raised new questions with regard to church-state problems—or, more precisely, have raised the old questions in a new form. Both the Economic Opportunity Act of 1964 and the Elementary and Secondary Education Act of 1965 serve these laudable purposes, but in drafting them Congress, in an effort to find some kind of a workable compromise, seems to have relied to some extent at least upon the child-benefit theory. The danger exists, therefore, that in the administration of these programs public money will seep into nonpublic agencies and schools, including parochial schools, in constitutionally impermissible ways.

The first of these Acts, for example, provides for the establishment of Job Corps Centers to offer education, training, and constructive work experience to impoverished young men and women, sixteen through twenty-one; provides work-training programs (the Neighborhood Youth Corps) in hospitals, settlement houses, both public and parochial schools, libraries, courts, parks, and playgrounds; provides part-time employment opportunities both on and off campus for college and university students; establishes special youth programs in impoverished areas; provides substantial aid to communities desiring to mobilize their resources into action programs; offers special pre-school experience for deprived children (Project Headstart); establishes programs of instruction to decrease illiteracy among adults; provides assistance of several kinds to low income and migrant agricultural workers; and establishes a domestic Peace Corps of volunteers to participate in a variety of antipoverty programs.

Administrative guidelines and policy directives specifically forbid that any of these programs involve work on church buildings and property owned by religious institutions, work that will free and thus subsidize others to perform these services, and work on any facility used for sectarian instruction or religious worship. The law itself, under Title II (Community Action Programs), demands that "No grant or contract authorized under this part may provide for general aid to elementary or secondary education in any school or school system." Nevertheless, questionable contracts have been written with parochial school agencies, including schools, for the use of various kinds of facilities, opportunities for discrimination against nonparochial school participants can be observed through various loopholes (and have actually appeared in places as far apart as Philadelphia and Tacoma), and at least one of the Titles, in the words of the minority of the House Education Committee, "is completely wide open to the use of funds for sectarian purposes."

The situation with respect to the Elementary and Secondary Education Act is similar. Again laudable in purpose, the Act would do a great deal for educationally deprived children, strengthen library facilities in American communities, and stimulate educational innovation. Again, however, certain compromises were made and various ambiguities appear, ambiguities that some writers fear "may lead to a vitriolic and irresponsible community conflict." The Act provides substantial sums to public schools in low income areas for projects which must then be made available to all educationally deprived children in the area, whether public or parochial school pupils; provides substantial sums also for the acquisition of school library resources, textbooks, and other printed materials for the use of children and teachers in public and private elementary and secondary schools (the child-benefit theory becomes explicit here); provides mobile services and equipment which may be used on private school premises; and establishes supplementary educational centers for educational innovation and experiment which include private as well as public agencies.

The Act, of course, contains certain safeguards against the growth of unconstitutional practices. Like the poverty program, however, the education program is susceptible to several kinds of abuse, including (1) discrimination on religious grounds; (2) seepage of public funds into religious organizations; (3) use of public funds to encourage church membership; and (4) transference of public control to private religious bodies. Although the legislation is federal, the programs themselves operate on local levels where prohibitions written into the law can be attenuated by local sentiment or by local negligence. Only local vigilance, therefore, can prevent abuses which would at first slowly and then with accelerating speed erode the principle of separation of church and state.[2]

The programs and practices mentioned so far concern for the most part federal aid to elementary and secondary education. Some hold that the problems involved in giving federal aid to higher education are different from the ones involved in giving federal aid to education at a lower level. Others maintain that the issues are exactly the same. Adherents of the former view base their case on considerations outlined in a memorandum prepared by the Department of Health, Education, and Welfare entitled "The Impact of the First Amendment to the Constitution Upon Federal Aid to Education," which indicated basic differences, as follows:

> We are not, at the college level, dealing with a system of universal, free, compulsory education available to all students. The process is more selective, the education more specialized, and the role of private institutions vastly more important. There are obvious limitations upon what the Government can hope to accomplish by way of expanding public or other secular educational facilities. If the public purpose is to be achieved at all, it can only be achieved by a general expansion of private as well as public colleges, of sectarian as well as secular ones.

The opposing point of view is well expressed by the ACLU of Southern California which reminds us that the First Amend-

[2] That some of these abuses have in fact occurred is the conclusion of a recent study by George LaNoue, a preliminary report of which appeared in *Civil Liberties*, May 1968, p. 5.

ment "draws no distinction with reference to religion for children, religion for those of college age, and religion for adults; its ban against federal support of religion applies to all indiscriminately."

The problem here rests upon the fact that although most private colleges and universities were founded under religious auspices and even now sometimes require representatives of religious groups on their boards of trustees, many of them are nevertheless wholly secular in their orientation and dedicate their endeavors to the pursuit of truth in the largest sense, a sense that altogether transcends sectarian limitations. In origin, for example, Columbia was Anglican, Harvard Unitarian, Princeton Presbyterian, and Chicago Baptist. We confront a situation here in which origin was religious but in which religious control has entirely disappeared and in which operation and purpose are as secular as they are in the great public universities. Certain other private universities, on the contrary, like Notre Dame, Fordham, Holy Cross, Brigham Young, Mercer (Baptist, of Georgia), and St. John's (Catholic, of New York), continue to function in ways that encourage the propagation and practice of a particular faith. Is it possible to distinguish, logically and pragmatically, between these two kinds of private institutions, the one qualified for federal aid and the other disqualified? The problem is aggravated by the fact that private colleges and universities, even the best endowed, are increasingly dependent upon various forms of federal assistance, without which some of them might immediately succumb and all of them ultimately disappear from the American scene.

Certain prescriptions, not yet tested, may help to solve the problem. First of all, of course, one would insist and reiterate that no public funds can be used, directly or indirectly, to aid or support any institution the educational program of which even remotely fosters religion through instruction, practice, exercise, or curricular requirement. Secondly, however, one may ask whether the college or university is wholly secular or partly religious. If it is wholly secular in its arrangements, pat-

terns, and activities, then there is little reason to deny it federal assistance on religious grounds. The difficulty, of course,
occurs in producing evidence that will support the judgment.
The bland assertion that the faculty is dedicated to the pursuit of truth without religious encumbrance, prejudice, or
preference does not suffice. The question must rather be asked
whether there is anything about the program of the college or
university which confuses or blurs the line that separates
church and state. If the answer is clearly and patently in the
negative then there is no reason to disqualify the institution
for the receipt of public funds. If the answer is in the affirmative, in no matter how microscopic a respect, public contributions become insupportable.

Some of the practices that would place an institution in the
latter category can be enumerated as follows: (1) if faculty
members are required to be adherents of a particular religion
or required to subscribe to any belief or faith as a condition of
appointment or promotion; (2) if students confront similar
requirements for admission or graduation; (3) if any student
or faculty member is required to attend religious services or
participate in religious programs; (4) if any student is required to register for a course in religion or to attend any
classes which foster religious doctrines; (5) if any student is
subject to disciplinary measures for violation of religious rules
(two students in a Catholic university, otherwise qualified,
were once denied the B.A. degree because they were married
in a civil ceremony); and (6) if instruction or educational activity is conducted in classrooms displaying religious symbols,
pictures, or objects.

It should be noted that none of these criteria prevents the
offering of courses in the history or sociology of religion, in
the literature of the world's religions, or in comparative religion. None of these, for that matter, prevents the existence in
a university of a department of religion, in which courses of
this kind are concentrated, provided, of course, that all doctrines are presented as items of knowledge and not as packets
of "truth," and provided also that the officers of instruction in

the department satisfy the same standards of scholarly competence that are applied to the members of other departments.
On the other hand, no theological seminary, no matter how
distinguished its faculty was, could qualify.

It seems possible, in short, to maintain the distinction mentioned earlier between teaching religion on the one hand and
teaching about religion on the other, to distinguish between
colleges and universities which engage in the former and
those which do not, and to justify the expenditure of public
funds for institutions of higher education in which the principle of the separation of church and state is neither abridged
nor threatened. It is not a purist position, to be sure, and distinctions may even be difficult in particular cases (especially
in a period when some Catholic colleges and universities are
moving in the direction of lay control), but it is one which
can perhaps command the reasonable assent of those who are
interested both in the future of private higher education in
the United States and in the safety of civil liberties.

The question of tax exemption for religious organizations,
including church property, is a troublesome one and the
Union has no clear policy on it. It has been urged by some
that if shared time programs are unconstitutional as an indirect aid to religion, tax exemption is a fortiori forbidden because it is a direct aid. It has been argued on the other hand
that the principle of separation requires tax exemption because to do otherwise is to interfere with the independence of
religion and to interfere, to that extent, with the free exercise
thereof. The present exemption, in this light, helps to preserve
the independence of both church and state and guarantees
their separation. There is some support in the Union for a
third view that, whatever the merits of the issue, tax exemption for religious organizations is so firmly entrenched in our
tradition that we would be tilting at windmills if we tried to
tamper with it. It was Oliver Wendell Holmes, Jr., who observed that a page of history is worth a volume of logic. It is
also worth a volume of law.

It has sometimes been asked whether the provision for chaplains of the various religious faiths in the armed services is not in fact a violation of the First Amendment. The answer to this question is in the negative for a very special reason. Persons who belong to the armed services, whether voluntarily or by conscription, come under military command and no longer have the freedom which their civilian compatriots enjoy. The state, under these circumstances, denies to them the free exercise of religion, a denial for which it can compensate by offering the opportunity for religious services and counseling in the form of military chaplains. The Union supports this answer but adds that such services, as sometimes happens, cannot constitutionally be extended to the families of servicemen who voluntarily accompany them to military installations, whether at home or abroad.

This is not to say that there are no problems in this area. Practices that are clearly unconstitutional continue to occur in the armed services, attributable in large part to the unexamined assumption that if religion is good, compulsory religion is even better. Every Sunday morning, for example, the cadets at the military academies—Army, Navy, and Air Force—dutifully fall in and march to chapel by order of the commandants, some of them to an interdenominational Protestant service, some to a Catholic one, and a smaller number to a Jewish one. This practice has stimulated a number of complaints, especially at the Air Force Academy, not only from some of the cadets who think that this is a vain and hollow way of introducing religion into their lives, but also from officials of the Lutheran Church who object to compulsory worship of any kind. The academies rationalize this practice in various ways by saying, for example, that they are responsible not only for the professional education of their charges but also for their moral development, that future officers must be able to appreciate the importance of religion to the men who will later come under their command, and that religion is the very foundation of morality and honor of which it is the business of the academies to instill.

None of these rationalizations, however, can withstand the force of the First Amendment because they violate both of its clauses. Compulsory chapel at a military academy, supported by public funds, establishes religion on the one hand and prevents its free exercise on the other. On this practice, furthermore, there is another prohibition in the body of the Constitution itself. Article VI provides without equivocation that "no religious test shall ever be required as a qualification to an office or public trust under the United States." If a commission in the armed services is such an office or public trust—and no one doubts that it is—then the answer is clear. By issuing an order to march to chapel the commandants of the academies offend the Constitution of the United States, a document they are sworn to uphold.

To an earnest and devoted disciple of a particular faith the position of the American Civil Liberties Union on many of the questions treated in this chapter must seem to be one of hostility to religion. To him religion (his own) is a good thing, indeed a necessary and a cherished thing, and any rule that restricts its practice and propagation must appear to him to be an evil thing. But that, of course, is precisely the point. The pluralistic society of the United States contains many religions, most of them theistic and some nontheistic. Each of them believes that it possesses the one truth and each of them must, in the American system, be permitted to indulge in its belief. But no one of them, in view of our historic principles, can be allowed to impose its faith upon those people of different beliefs. The ACLU defends both the free exercise of religion and the interdiction of its state-induced establishment.

There are few things about which men disagree with such fervor and intensity as their religious beliefs. On these disagreements and differences the state must have nothing to say. No one can be free to answer for himself the important and poignant questions of human life and destiny if any agency of the government can decide for him what rituals to practice, what ceremonies to observe, and what creeds to profess. Americans of intellect and good will—and of all faiths —have decided that their government should not use its awesome powers to support one religion in preference to others, all religions in preference to none, and none in preference to some. The Government of the United States, in harmony with its Constitution, must forever maintain a neutral stance, protecting the free exercise of religion wherever it appears, and prohibiting its establishment whenever it threatens. Only in this way can every citizen practice his religion in isolation or in concert as he desires, without fear that his government will intervene. Only in this way can he be assured that the same rights of religious freedom that are guaranteed to him are guaranteed also to those who disagree with him. It is this precious right of the individual, in an area that affects the very source and destiny of his being, to which the First Amendment to the Constitution is dedicated. It is a dedication also to which the American Civil Liberties Union is proud to subscribe.

# I V

# FREEDOM ON
# THE CAMPUS *

## by LOUIS M. HACKER

Even in a well-established democratic society, the free institutions of men—the rights to conscience, speech, the press, association—from time to time fall under attack, sometimes in-
termittently, sometimes with unrelenting pressure. But in a
democratic—unlike the totalitarian—world, one can fight back
in an effort to mobilize opinion, legislative sanction, and judi-

* The discussion here, written in September, 1967, has to do with academic freedom in colleges and universities. The two terms are used
interchangeably. When "independent college" is employed, the reference
is to such institutions as Amherst, Colgate, Smith, where usually only
an undergraduate degree is given.

Occasionally, the writer, without quotation marks, has used the exact
wording from the various policy statements on academic freedom issued by the American Civil Liberties Union's Academic Freedom Committee and approved by the parent organization's Board of Directors.
He has felt free to do so because of his long chairmanship of the Academic Freedom Committee and his active participation in the drawing
up of the statements during that period. But for the whole of this he
alone takes responsibility. [*Editor*]

cial approval in defense of what has come to be regarded as inalienable rights. One must not assume that the assault on liberty always originates with the vicious and the corrupt; differences about expressions of loyalty and the means by which survival can be achieved often are honest differences; and in times of peril the argument that the sanctity and privacy of the individual must be invaded to protect the national security has an attractive if not a compelling quality.

The great debate about liberty is founded upon the assumption that the truth will prevail given the openness of the channels of communication and the willingness of men—and their rationality is taken as axiomatic—to yield to persuasion. But what if there are two contesting forms of "truth," particularly if the means for its accomplishment are diametrically opposed—will men then give way before each other and reach a working and amicable consensus? The libertarian, following John Stuart Mill, must believe they will.

Academic freedom, in this sense, must be seen as part and parcel of the broader question of liberty and the safeguarding of civil liberties. In the United States exactly because higher education has always had a much broader base than in Britain and on the European continent; indeed, part of the American assumption is that the opportunities for higher education must be made as generally available to all those with capacity as in the case of secondary education—attempts to regulate and control faculties and disciplines and to weed out dissidents have not been uncommon. Higher education is in the public domain and not the prescriptive right of a few; those who have achieved it are not an elite from whom the civil service, the diplomatic corps, the ministry are automatically drawn; in consequence, legislative bodies and their committees, patriotic societies, civil and church groups of one kind or another feel free to scrutinize, criticize, and occasionally ask for control of curricula in colleges and universities and the interests and activities of teachers and students.

The fact that so much of higher education is being publicly supported (and for this reason is vulnerable) is really beside the point. Higher education on the European continent and, more recently, increasingly in Britain, too, is dependent upon public funds; and certainly in Europe and Britain the fierce white light of publicity that exposes to examination (and censure) American universities, their faculties, and their students is less frequently encountered.

By the same token, in the United States, organizations to defend academic freedom (and civil liberties, generally) have arisen, are being heard, and, what is even more important, are able to establish formal codes that set out clearly rights and responsibilities. Within the past half century there have appeared powerful bodies like the American Civil Liberties Union, the Association of American University Professors, the Association of American Colleges, the American Council on Education, the National Student Association, the American Political Science Association, the Association of American Law Schools, which have been constantly on the alert to expose efforts at restriction on the one hand and to formulate procedures to establish due process for those under attack on the other.

When such codes are accepted—by university governing bodies, administrative officers, and faculties—then rules of law, in effect, have been established. To this extent, despite recurrent efforts to limit the freedom of universities and their members, academic freedom in the United States has been strengthened and recognized (although not yet everywhere; not yet in many Catholic institutions of higher learning) because rights and responsibilities have been defined.

All of this has grown out of the diversity of American experiences in the complex pattern of American higher education; of equal significance, despite the persistence of the Jacksonian tradition of the full equality of all persons, has been a growing awareness of the larger role higher education has been playing in America and the insistence on the part of teachers—and more recently on the part of students—that academic persons have the private rights of citizens: to participate politically, to petition, to run uncensored forums where all manner of opinions may be aired.

Under the influence of the Enlightenment toward the end of the eighteenth century, in the few American colleges then in existence, the general idea of intellectual freedom (which went hand in hand with toleration and religious liberty) was being accorded recognition—with many reservations, of course. (Even Thomas Jefferson, for example, was not certain that his political opponents, the Federalists, ought to teach law in the University of Virginia.) There was a setback in the following half century because the Romantic reaction to the Enlightenment and the spread of sectarian (and authoritarian) particularism—most of the new colleges appearing were under denominational auspices—put orthodoxy as the first test of competence. The curricula were still largely classical (or medieval) in character, and the lesser part played by natural science, with its rigorous emphasis on experimentation and verification, checked the widespread demand for and acceptance of those rights of free and fearless inquiry which are the hallmarks of the academic world today. Professors and college presidents in this earlier time not infrequently were brought to book—by self-perpetuating boards of trustees—for heterodoxies of one kind or another; they resigned or were discharged; and just as often they could find havens in other institutions where their beliefs were acceptable.

After the American Civil War, the triumph of Darwinism over Revelation had two consequences: it raised the study of science to an equal place with the humanities, and it weakened the authority of lay (and clerical) governing bodies. Interestingly enough, academic freedom (in the collegiate sense, wholly) was accorded first to the students: to choose their courses of study (including scientific ones), to elect individual subjects, and to absent themselves from chapel attendance.

There were other forces at work to strengthen the claims of the scholar to independence: he was in process of becoming professionalized (he attended a graduate school, he belonged to a learned society); he required more elaborate tools in carrying out his function (laboratories, libraries); he was participating more and more in the world at large as consultant, expert, and adviser to public authorities. Not the least of the influences was the impact of the German universities to which thousands of young Americans were streaming and whose educational principles, in part, at any rate, they sought to establish in the American universities, the ones that is, with strong graduate departments, which were then emerging—Johns Hopkins, Clark, Stanford, Chicago, Cornell, Columbia, Harvard. In Germany *Lehrfreiheit* (that professors were free to examine students and adjudge their competence, to lecture and publish in their subjects without let or hindrance) was encountered, admired, and transplanted into American universities. The *Lernfreiheit* of German students (that they were under no restraints in the learning process; all they had to do was to submit themselves for the final examination) was something else again: the American students were still being regarded as subjects for guidance and discipline.

The right to inquire, test, reject, or asseverate by university members certainly became increasingly true of the natural sciences and the humanities. In the social sciences—where the questions raised sometimes touched on public policy (immigration, taxation) or the conduct of a market consumer (trade union recognition, trusts, minimum wages, consumer protection)—the unorthodox ran the risk of criticism or even dismissal. Between the 1880's and the end of World War I not a few such cases arose; usually the pressures came from the outside—from the benefactors of the great new universities making their appearance, or from businessmen or their associations. Again, however, an academic who had fallen into disfavor could, as a rule, find a place elsewhere; the prevailing conservatism in the social sciences was not due to a reign of terror but was a characteristic of the general modes of thinking and acceptance.

In the first half of the 1950's—it will always be known as the McCarthy Era—the scrutiny and the criticism of the aca-

demic world came from another direction: from legislative
bodies and their committees, in both houses of Congress and,
in many states, and from patriotic organizations. Fearful over
the national security (these were the years of the "cold" war
and the Korean War), they were concerned not as much with
nonorthodoxy in the classroom as they were with outside association and activity. The assumptions were that security
would be achieved if loyalty was publicly proclaimed (by loyalty oaths, too many of them vague and all-encompassing),
past derelictions (no matter how remote) confessed, and
present conformity (in and out of the classrooms) used as the
test for competency and integrity instead of the judgment of
one's peers.

The McCarthy years were difficult years, because teachers
particularly were singled out for attack. Many teachers, their
loyalty questioned, were examined by the McCarthy Committee and by similar state legislative bodies. Sometimes university administrative action alone, based solely on the publication of the names of teachers under scrutiny or because of
their appearance before such committees, took the form of
dismissals, forced resignations, and withheld promotions.
Teachers who, in their youth, had for brief periods deliberately or unwittingly been associated with the Communist
party or its front organizations, and who, as a matter of conscience, refused to name those who had been involved in such
groups or activities with them were not only dismissed but
were, and sometimes remained, permanently blacklisted.
Numbers of teachers who had never violated the integrity of
the classroom or their commitment as honest scholars were
thereby lost to the profession.

The McCarthy years took a heavy toll of teachers and some
of the consequences continued to flare up occasionally in the
1960's. Certainly in the 1950's there was a definite decline in
intellectual and academic freedom. The esteem of teachers in
the eyes of the outside world sank to a low point. Many
teachers withdrew from participation in social, political, and
economic associations and discussions. Some admitted that

they resorted to precautionary devices in classrooms and in their writings to allay criticism, censure, and the threat of dismissal. Moreover, in a number of states, laws were enacted requiring teachers to take loyalty oaths, and in not a few, demanding statements of earlier association with so-called subversive organization. Not until the second half of the 1960's did the U.S. Supreme Court begin to examine—and reject—these widesweeping loyalty oaths and declarations.

So much for the efforts to crib, cabin, and confine teachers and their activities in and out of the classroom. A similar situation existed in the case of students. Right up to the middle 1960's, it was widely held that teachers and notably student deans stood in *loco parentis* to students. High jinks, no matter how destructive, might be permissible within the precincts of the college ("boys will be boys"), but attempts to participate politically, in and out of the college, by demonstrations, petitions, strikes or boycotts of classes, were something else again. These were outside the range of student rights.

Legislative bodies have (and should have in a democracy) great authority. Patriotic organizations, like all groups of citizens, have the right to scrutinize and discuss whatever goes on in an open society. As long as legislative mandates are not too vague and scrutiny and discussion do not end in threats and intimidation, individual freedoms are not in permanent jeopardy.

But legislative inquiry and statutory restriction make up one side of the coin; dismissing professors and students for political belief and activity is, however, the other. On the matter of the subversion of the state (once it is defined by the courts) or the perversion of the academic process in the classroom there is no quarrel. Communists (for this is really what everyone is talking about—or was in the 1950's!) who are overtly or covertly conspiratorial have no claims on academic freedom, for they themselves would be the first to abridge or abolish it once they were in power. The point is, who shall do the dismissing, and for what reasons?

It is here that the clearest thinking has taken place and the clearest gains made. Thanks to the pioneering efforts of the American Association of University Professors as early as 1915, the position of the teacher (but not of the student) was sharply defined. Said the report of the Association's Committee on Academic Freedom and Tenure: "The liberty of the scholar within the university to set forth his conclusions, be they what they may, is conditioned by their being conclusions gained by a scholar's method and held in a scholarly spirit. . . ." The scholar had all the ordinary rights of a citizen outside the university, always assuming that he would act with discretion and awareness of his university affiliation.

In 1940, the American Association of University Professors and the Association of American Colleges (speaking for presidents and deans) signed jointly a somewhat similar statement calling upon American colleges to endorse a declaration that approved of academic freedom in the classroom and freedom for the teacher outside it. How to assure these rights, however? Here, the American Civil Liberties Union, which has played such an important role in the safeguarding of citizens' rights against oppressive law enforcement authorities, courts, legislative bodies, and civic organizations, led the way. As early as 1925, the ACLU had begun to preoccupy itself with problems of academic freedom, and it had issued a series of notable reports. In 1952, and in greater detail in 1954—this was during the McCarthy Era—the ACLU worked out carefully a set of rules to assure what it called the establishment of "academic due process."

The ACLU said flatly that the "central issue, in considering a teacher's fitness, is his performance in his subject and his relationship to his students. . . . In the absence of substantial evidence of perversion of the academic process, the ACLU opposes the prohibition in educational employment of any person based even in part on his views or associations, such as Communist or Fascist." And who were the judges of "substantial evidence of perversion of the academic process" to be? They were to be one's peers, "a committee of colleagues in an academic hearing."

The procedural rules (to assure due process) were spelled out in great detail. Universities should create a standing committee or a special committee of faculty members exclusively, before which such hearings were to be held. The accused was entitled to counsel, a statement of written charges, the right of confrontation of hostile witnesses and their cross-examination, and the preparation of a formal record. And the ACLU ended: "In the absence of a defect in procedure, the conclusions of the hearing committee should be taken as final by the administration and governing body in all matters relating to the teacher's competence and integrity." In the event of a finding unfavorable to the teacher, machineries for appeal were to be established and could be invoked.

Following the same lines, the American Association of University Professors and the Association of American Colleges, in 1958, reached an agreement for the creation of instrumentalities of due process in which administrative officers and governing bodies were to be only complainants and not at the same time prosecutor, judge, and jury. Many colleges and universities, by formal faculty participation, adopted the code or one similar to it; and to this extent, despite investigations, charges of failure to "cooperate," occasional demands for loyalty oaths and for the dismissal of persons under fire, legal procedures became increasingly common practice.

The ACLU, too, led the way in the case of adumbrating and defending student rights. Its first statement, called "Academic Freedom and Civil Rights of Students," appeared in 1956. There, it insisted that the then held conception of the wardship of the student (and the surrogate role of the university) had to be abandoned. Students should be allowed a free press, free forums, free association, and the rights of demonstration and participation in outside political activities; due process, too, should be established when disciplinary action might entail suspension or expulsion; and difficulties with civil authorities where off-campus political matters were involved were outside the area of university responsibility and penalties.

On the campus, "regulations governing the extracurricular activities of students should be enacted, amended, and supplemented, and penalties for violation thereof imposed, by a committee composed of faculty members and students." Such regulations were to be fully publicized. Again, the request was for the formulation and adoption of, in effect, legal codes (with students also represented on hearing bodies when charges of violation were made) in which rights and responsibilities were set out and duly observed. Unhappily, as far as students were concerned, too few colleges did so: hence the turmoil on American campuses in the 1960's.

To repeat an earlier statement here: academic freedom is part and parcel of the broader question of liberty and the safeguarding of civil liberties. More particularly, academic freedom (and academic responsibility) may be defined as the liberty and obligation to study, to investigate, to hypothesize about, to present and interpret, and to discuss facts and ideas concerning all fields of learning. No limitations are implied other than those required by generally accepted standards of responsible scholarship.

Academic freedom does not merely denote rights which are reserved to members of the academic community in the event that they choose to exercise them. Unless they are exercised there is no academic freedom. An academic community has an obligation to test constantly the received opinions and institutions of its time and society in addition to opening up and exploring new frontiers of knowledge, and to nurture free intellects to carry on both tasks. To this extent, part of the academic freedom of students is their "right to know," to raise questions when they think curricula are inadequate or departments in their instruction are following a line of tendency that excludes other viewpoints or modes of analysis.

Outside the academic community, teachers and students should have no less freedom than other citizens. The teacher, because of his profession, is not required to remain silent as a price of professorial status, nor the student because of fear of dismissal or suspension. On the contrary, the teacher's position imposes upon him the two-fold duty of advancing new and useful ideas and of examining any doctrine which may be outworn. However, since the public may judge his profession and his institution by his utterances, he should not only maintain high professional excellence but also make clear that he does not represent the institution of which he is a part. When he speaks, writes, or acts as an individual, he should be free from institutional censorship or discipline.

It is similar in the case of the student, when his outside activities involve him with law-enforcement authorities in matters of conscience. He should not be put in double jeopardy and disciplinary action should not be taken against him for engaging in such off-campus matters as political campaigns, picketing, the participation in public demonstrations. He should not, of course, speak in the name of his college or one of its general student organizations.

Students may be arrested for taking part in such activities, broadly, in what may be denominated political offenses. Students who may violate a local ordinance or any law which they consider to be morally wrong risk the legal penalties prescribed by the civil authorities. Since not every conviction under law is for an offense with which an educational institution must concern itself, it is important that college authorities refrain from administrative decisions which would violate the students' academic freedom.

A further caution: a record of arrest is not a conviction, whatever the transgression. Even when criminal offenses have been committed, judgment should be suspended until the student has exhausted every legal remedy available to him. When the offenses are political and students have run into police difficulties off the campus in connection with civil rights, war protests, or labor demonstrations, college authorities should, ideally, take every practical step to assure themselves that such students are protected in their full legal rights if not in the name of the college itself, certainly through individual faculty, student, or alumni groups.

Unless college authorities act in behalf of students, there is the very real danger of alienation: of the weakening of confidence in the university as a community and the resort to outside agencies—some of which may very well be self-serving—for support and defense. College authorities have as much responsibility for maintaining that community—based upon mutual trust, respect, and forbearance—as do teachers and students.

The rights and responsibilities of teachers as citizens are clear enough and scarcely need be further developed here. They are those of other citizens. For this reason disclaimer affidavits or negative oaths—that one is not or never has been a member of such and such an organization, whether proscribed or not—carry the aura of suspicion and are an affront to the profession and the individual. The same is true of positive oaths—pledging allegiance to country or state and its existing institutions, and the like—when teachers are singled out to do so as conditions prior to employment or public financial aid. All oaths, even for public officials or employees alone, are silly and useless and might well be dispensed with. There is cogency in the point that the state—public authority —is entitled to the loyalty of those who work for it; it is doubtful if an oath assures such loyalty or prevents those covertly engaged against the state from taking it. Certainly, singling out teachers, or other special bodies of employees or persons receiving financial aid, *e.g.*, students seeking public scholarships or fellowships under the National Defense Education Act, is invidious and in violation of their civil liberties.

Only one point in reference to the teacher as teacher needs further elaboration and that has to do with appointment and tenure.

Appointment should be made solely on the basis of teaching ability and competence in one's profession and without regard to such factors as race, sex, nationality, creed, religious or political belief or affiliation, or behavior not demonstrably related to the teaching profession. Appointments, when made at the lowest levels, should be recommended by the appropriate departments; where tenure is involved, by the relevant departments and faculties.

Temporary appointments—tutors, teaching assistants, instructors, assistant professors, usually—should be clearly defined, their terms limited, and sufficient notice of intention not to reappoint given so that the appointee may make other plans for employment.

Tenure appointments—usually associate professors and professors—whether made from the outside or through promotion inside, require further safeguards. A department alone, lest it continue a line of tendency too narrowly restrictive and consequent inbreeding, should welcome the participation of members of the faculty of which it is a part, where allied interests are represented. The best device is an *ad hoc* committee to which might well be named one or more professors from other universities: such appointments or promotions having been recommended, administrative veto must be explained and discussed; in no case should it be exercised as a *dictat*. The recent occurrence (April, 1967) at the (Catholic) American University in Washington is a case in point. An assistant professor of theology was recommended for promotion (and tenure) to an associate professorship by his department and faculty. The governing board vetoed this and in fact ordered that he be dropped at the end of the academic year. A strike of students and professors, in which members of the whole university participated, was necessary before the governing body reconsidered, reinstated the professor, and accepted the promotion.

What of proprietary or church-affiliated institutions with close denominational identification? Even here, the interests and wishes of departments and faculties should be overriding; the intervention of administrative officials and boards of trustees is fraught with danger and is becoming increasingly repugnant to self-respecting academics. The values of academic freedom and responsibility as here defined are likely to serve the best interests of educational institutions—to have the respect of the public, the world of learning, the students —even when presumably distinctive purposes, whether set forth in charters or by long usage, are involved.

What of teaching versus research? This question is likely to be raised more often by students than by academic personnel themselves. Students from time to time seek to engage in the processes of faculty evaluation—there should be no objection to such exercises and to their publication; from time to time they protest against the failure to renew the appointments or to make the promotions of popular teachers, popular because of a good presence in the classroom or because a large amount of time is spent with and over the affairs and concerns of students, whether these involvements are educational or personal. Such manifestations of interest on the part of students should be given courteous attention and the reasons for the action taken, vis-à-vis nonreappointment or failure to promote, fully explained. Talking out a problem, arranging for the maintenance of regular lines of communication, is likely to dispel hostility and clear away suspicion that personalities or political views and conduct are involved rather than the best interests of the university community.

On the basis of such discussions, a department may want to re-examine the reasons it has used for failure to reappoint; or it may decide to extend the probationary period. Or its explanations for its course of action may reassure students. Bold universities may want to experiment with student advisory committees (from those majoring in a department? or taking honors?) to be regularly assembled when sticky matters of the kind referred to come up. In any event, ultimate decisions must rest where they should in matters of selection of teaching staff, curriculum, individual courses, sequences of study: with departments, faculties, academic deans. A student-run university where students have been allowed to exercise vetoes on educational matters (which has been attempted from time to time in Latin-American and Asian countries) is a disaster, and the students are the losers.

It is doubtful if a real dichotomy exists between teaching

and research and that a small independent college best serves students and the public by appointing "teachers" rather than "scholars." A man fully *au courant* in his field of learning, contributing to it by his own researches and writings—whether in a small college or a large university—ends up by being the better teacher, even if he is not a spectacular performer in the classroom. Great scholars by choice have remained in small colleges—and by their presence attracted good students and the public regard for their institutions. Scholarship is not measured quantitatively but qualitatively; students sometimes assume the former, but they are in error. Whatever the immediate problems, free and full discussion clears the air and maintains mutual confidence.

When administrative officials or boards of trustees act summarily by discharging teachers with temporary appointments or tenure—or force retirement of tenure teachers—they are violating academic due process. This subject requires fuller attention and to it we now turn.

We are taking for granted that fitness to teach is based upon competence and integrity. The latter includes the creation and maintenance in the classroom of a spirit of free inquiry. This does not mean that the teacher may not hold views of his own and present them; if he clearly marks them as his, the students are in a better position to appraise his judgments and differ from them on the basis of other materials to which they have been exposed. A tendentious position, labeled "objective" scholarship, throws into question the teacher's integrity; and there is no defense—certainly the ACLU would not provide one—of a teacher discharged after proof has been adduced of his misuse of his position to pervert the academic process. Membership alone in religious, dogmatic, or politically authoritarian groups is no proof per se. Nor is the refusal to testify before a legislative committee proof. The *sine qua non* is the individual himself in his academic and intellectual relations with his colleagues, his broad field of scholarship, and his students.

If these and other questions arise in which the teacher's position qua teacher is involved, academic due process must be invoked because academic freedom is the issue.

The university, its whole community of students and alumni, the teacher involved in an academic freedom case, will want to avoid undue publicity. It is true that if academic due process is not being observed, an appeal to public opinion may represent the only possible course for the reaching of a fair judgment.

Due process assumes, at any rate under Anglo-Saxon law and practice, that a person charged is innocent until proved guilty and that the burden of proof rests upon the accusers. Through the centuries, courts have applied these notions in the formulation of legal due process and they should operate with equal force in academic due process. The responsibility for applying these principles in the world of education is that of the governing body and the administration of an institution.

Put briefly and broadly, academic due process entails the following: charges made against a teacher should be explicit, supported by evidence, and furnished him; they should be presented before a committee (standing or *ad hoc*) of his peers chosen by the faculty and from the faculty; the teacher charged should have the right to counsel, to confront witnesses, and a full opportunity to deny, refute, and rebut evidence; a record of the proceeding is to be kept, and the teacher, if adjudged guilty, does not waive his rights to further appeal to a state commissioner of education or to the courts. Some of these matters require further elucidation.

Informal procedures, however, are best in order to avoid jeopardizing the career of the teacher and the reputation of the institution. Whether the agreed-upon method is face-to-face confrontation and discussion, or third-party conciliation or mediation or arbitration, or the invited participation of an organization interested in academic freedom, a solution may be arrived at without the engendering of ill will in the academic community or a hue and cry raised outside it. The informal presentation of the administration's viewpoint, through one or all of these methods, may persuade a teacher to recognize his duty to cooperate with his institution and to indicate how he may do so without sacrifice of principle. Exposition of the teacher's viewpoint may persuade the administration not to challenge his competence and integrity. If these procedures are not tried or if they fail, a formal hearing is in order.

When may suspension take place? It should occur in the case of a teacher holding tenure only when serious violation of law or public moral conduct is admitted or proved before a competent court. It may occur if indictments by a grand jury or information handed up by a district attorney will lead to court trials. It should not occur as a result of charges made by, or refusal to testify before, a legislative committee. In any event, suspension should be accompanied by full pay; and such suspension should continue until the academic community of which the teacher is a member decides for itself whether the outside legal action is relevant to his continuance as a teacher.

Now, as to the intramural hearing. The university hearing committee, either a standing committee or an *ad hoc* one, should be set by up pre-established rules. It should be democratically chosen from the full-time teaching staff. It should name its chairman from its own members. The administration should not seek to influence the hearing committee except through argument presented openly before it.

Such a hearing committee should be deemed as having an advisory role. But in the absence of defects in procedure, the counsel of wisdom would be for the administration and governing body to accept as final the judgment concerning the teacher's competence and integrity and his continuance as a teacher in good standing and without prejudice. However, if the judgment is unfavorable to the teacher, he should have the right to appeal to the governing body, to the state commissioner of education, and to the civil courts.

It is strongly urged that the whole dispute—the charges, the countercharges, the judgment—be kept within the family, that is, the educational world, where rights, responsibilities, competence, integrity, are fully understood, evaluative tests have been formulated, and extraneous matters can be eliminated without rancor or heat. If the state commissioner of education, who does have authority over both public and private educational institutions, is a man of proved educational capacity (and not chosen by the legislature or publicly elected) he is likely not to yield to outside pressures and the final appeal may well rest there. Resorting to the civil courts, particularly if they are state courts, runs into real dangers. Pressures, whether political or religious or ethnic, will be attempted; appeals to the national security (if the question has come up) will be made; the accused's political views and associations and personal habits (if they are heterodox or unconventional) will be dragged in, and the basic matters at issue will be lost or obscured in irrelevancies.

If the academic or educational world has established its *bona fides*, as it has in the United States, it should be permitted to decide who shall and who shall not continue in good standing in its own community.

With regard to nontenure teachers, American educational practice permits great fluidity in their testing as to the permanent usefulness of such teachers in a particular institution. It has already been observed that this period of probation should not be unduly prolonged and that if the decision not to renew a temporary contract is taken, adequate advance notice in writing should be given.

This experimental phase of a teacher's career is wisely characterized by a minimum of formal judgment; teachers come and go without recorded praise or blame. Also, nontenure appointments (as in night extension programs) often fall within the marginal area of an institution's educational and financial program; the dropping of a teacher may have no bearing whatsoever upon his professional capacity.

However, while letting such a teacher go does not necessarily raise an academic freedom question, in his mind such an issue may be present—that is to say, questions of race or religious belief or association may have been factors for non-retention. Such improper consideration is entitled to all the protection of academic due process. If the nonretained teacher feels—with appropriate advice—that he has proof to support his contention, he has the right to invoke the informal and/or formal procedures outlined above.

Many of the rights and responsibilities that teachers possess and assume should also be given to students in the same free academic climate. Today, notably, because students have become so deeply involved emotionally and actively in the problems troubling their elders—civil rights, the national role in the outside world, the United States at war although without a formal war declaration, poverty, the educational process—they have widened their areas of examination, discussion, and participation. The narrow, sheltered world of Academe no longer exists; and while youth has its own problems—the psychological and physical traumas of growing up; the necessity for adjusting to (or rejecting!) the larger commitments of the most powerful nation on the earth—it still has to carry on in the role of student in the traditional sense. Formal education is more important today than ever before because of great scientific and technological advances in the social as well as the natural sciences; indeed, the period of preparation for one's taking a place in such a complex society regularly lengthens.

But there is no real conflict. As Dean Erwin N. Griswold of the Harvard Law School wrote in 1961 (this was the time of student involvement in the struggle for civil rights):

A university is a place where students learn not merely from the past but also through developing the capacity for and habit of independent thought. If they are well taught, they learn to do their own thinking. There is no "party line" in any American university worthy of the name. Great ideas can rarely be developed in an atmosphere of constraint and oppression. The university has a

unique function not merely in systematizing the orthodox,
but also in providing the soil in which may be nourished
the speculative, the unfashionable, and the unorthodox.

The modern-day restiveness of students—occasioned in part
by their involvements outside the campus, in part by their
dissatisfactions (real or fancied) with what is taking place on
the campus in the management of the university and its educational practices—requires a further expansion of Dean Griswold's eloquent asseveration. Students ask that they be heard
and that they be allowed to participate in university decision
making on the broadest front.

All this is an area that, literally, a decade ago, was still terra
incognita. There will have to be a good deal of give and take,
experiments embarked on and proposals rejected but in an
atmosphere of mutual respect and trust!—until a fair relationship, conducive to the maintenance of the university as a vi-
able institution, is worked out between students and their
administrators and their teachers. The rights of students will
have to be re-examined and their responsibilities carefully defined and accepted by them.

A further observation. The great growth in physical size
and number of the American universities (and this applies
equally to independent colleges) has made the personal relation between student and teacher difficult to maintain. The
expanding world of scholarship and public service—the ease
with which the scholar of accomplishment can get financial
grants to take him *off* the campus; by the same token, the
ease with which he can get funds to do his own research or
work on government contracts *on* the campus—also attenu-
ates the possibilities of contact between student and teacher.
Government contracts (whether in pure or applied research)
frequently make unwilling captors or clients of postgraduate
students. To survive—as teaching assistants or the recipients
of financial aid—they are compelled to work on the bits and
pieces of projects or problems of their faculty supervisors
without the opportunity to pursue independent lines of in-

quiry. It is not surprising that these graduate students are most articulate and frequently are the initiators in voicing and formulating the discontents and leading the discontented on American campuses.

All this requires important changes in educational procedures. Only a few may be hinted at here. Classes will have to be smaller, whether by the establishment of semiautonomous colleges in the university (English-style; California is attempting this—a very costly reform) or by less of formal instruction in the classroom itself. Undergraduate students, possibly by the end of the first year, will have to be put on their own— equipped with elaborate courses of study whose requirements they will have to master—and then assembled, possibly in their last year, in small colloquia and seminars where students and teachers will be working together closely on advanced problems. Graduation and class rank will depend on final comprehensive (written and oral) examinations as at the Oxford and Cambridge undergraduate colleges.

But this puts a great burden on the secondary schools and thoroughgoing reforms here too will be necessary: to give students preparing for college complete command of those skills and tools—reading, writing, mathematics, scientific analysis and logical method, foreign languages—that college students in good part on their own will need.

And what of the teacher who is always off somewhere—in a retreat for academics, attending international conferences, advising foreign governments, or lecturing in foreign universities? Sometimes a book or a meaningful piece of research comes from these journeyings; too frequently, not. Universities will have to put restraints upon such goings and comings if the grievances of students—and their overall cynicism about the university's responsibilities to *them*—are to be allayed.

As for the postgraduate students, their captivity is nothing less than indecent. Financial assistance should have no strings attached—the professor may think his patronage (but the students' clientship!) is a friendly act; a thesis of sorts will be finished, a job will be obtained—for the intellectual inde-

pendence of the student is a bloom carefully to be nurtured.
To speed up the processes of postgraduate study and, by that
token, to make possible financial assistance without work for
money are important desiderata for the creation of respect
and the encouraging of fruitful exploration of ideas on the
part of postgraduate students. The Ford Foundation, in order
to accomplish exactly these things among others, has recently
embarked on a large program working with a representative
number of universities heavily committed to postgraduate
studies.

These are some of the matters that have to be cleared away
to obtain that mutual trust and respect so that university administrators, teachers, and students can live and work together.

In the light of what has already been said—to encourage
students to develop "the capacity for and habit of independent thought"; to help them make meaningful decisions in
their own lives and as citizens in a society based on law and
constitutional guarantees—one does not have to labor any
more the kind of things students may do on and off the
campus.

They should have freedom of expression in their student
organizations, clubs, and societies and, as individuals, to talk,
hear others talk, pass resolutions, draw up petitions, distribute
leaflets, post notices, demonstrate, and strike, if they think
such an extreme form of expression is necessary. They should
have the right to raise funds on the campus to finance their
interests, as long as fund raising is confined to student organizations and has for its purpose the support of recognized char-
itable organizations, public service agencies, and university
and university-related groups. There are several provisos.
Only accredited (who shall do the accrediting will be discussed
below) clubs and societies should engage in such fashion.
When individuals do so, *e.g.,* circulate petitions and distribute
leaflets, they should sign their names to indicate they are bona
fide students. Demonstrations and strikes should be peaceable
in much the same fashion as the civil authorities and the

courts define peaceable assembly. And only bona fide students may take part in demonstrations within the university precincts.

A caveat, however: demonstrators who deprive others of the opportunity to speak or be heard, or physically obstruct movement, or otherwise disrupt the normal educational or institutional processes (*e.g.*, preventing the university's guests from being received; preventing legitimate private organizations and public agencies from recruiting students for jobs or training) are violating academic freedom.

Granted, in times of sharp differences of opinion, as do exist today, some young people are moved by conscience to use extraordinary, even obstructive and violent means to achieve their particular ends, to create the university in *their* image. But they are denying the rights of others—they are engaging in acts of civil disobedience—and they must be prepared to accept the responsibility of their actions.

To clear the air, to make certain that there are rights and kindred responsibilities for the maintenance of an orderly society, regulations governing demonstrations need to be drawn up and fully publicized. And the same is true of the possible penalties that may be imposed. Such regulations should be made by administration and faculty in consultation with students; and when infractions are charged, students should be accorded the fullest protection of due process.

The word "responsibility" has been used here frequently; at this point, specificity is in order. "Responsibility" connotes a meaningful role in the legislative and judicial processes as they affect the living, acting, and transgressing of students on the campus. This requires, therefore, playing a part, along with administration and faculty, in drawing up the ground rules for living and receiving guests in dormitories; for dressing and grooming (if students think extreme or bizarre habits require regulation); for the sale and use of drugs by students; for accrediting student societies and organizations and other forms of student life; for the conduct of peaceable demonstrations; and for participating in the judicial process when infractions of rules occur. In this last connection, *i.e.*, observing all the requirements of due process, a properly elected dormitory council could very well act as a court of first instance to pass on infractions and recommend appropriate penalties, and possibly act also when it comes to such matters as cheating in examinations and plagiarism. In any event, these are areas where experimentation needs to take place for the purpose of widening the zone of responsibility.

It will not do, once responsibility has been accorded, for administration, faculty, or other students to protest that representative students or representative student bodies have been too harsh or too lax in the work of drawing up rules or sitting in judgment or that they have curbed the rights of minorities. As in the outside world where representatives are chosen, the electorate has one recourse: it can turn out incumbents in office and pick new ones. So it should be on the campus. As discussions take place, differences are aired, and the decision makers are persuaded to change their minds or are replaced by normal previously agreed-upon procedures.

Students should be free to join clubs and societies for educational, political, social, religious, or cultural purposes. The fact of affiliation with any extramural association or national organization or political party, so long as it is an open affiliation, should not of itself bar a group from recognition. Because recognition entails the employment of campus facilities—meeting and assembly rooms, halls and open places, the use of local mails and bulletin boards—a student-activities council (with or without faculty participation), democratically chosen, might well be given the right to accredit and withdraw accreditation for the violation of rules (previously drawn up) of performance and responsibility. Invitations to outside speakers, of whatever hue or persuasion, are within the rights of such accredited societies, and sufficient notice to the college administration that such invitations have been extended should be enough. On the other hand, it is up to the administration and its security office to see that such meetings are protected from invasion, and up to the chairman of the meeting to see that the proceeding is conducted with decorum. In this last, a faculty member, experienced in the conduct of such assemblies, would be the wisest choice to chair when a "controversial" speaker is to appear. Questions (but not statements) should be permitted from the floor.

And what if the speaker is "controversial"? Should students be warned—by faculty members and college administration?—that they are in danger of being led up the garden path? Today, this is scarcely necessary, for students know—or will be told at once by the outside press and their own—who so-and-so is and how dishonorable his intentions are. Often such invitations are extended simply for the purpose of seeing—and questioning and challenging!—people in the public eye, or testing the patience and forbearance of administrations, governing boards, alumni, and the outside world. The college president or dean of students may have to explain this again and again to governing boards, alumni, parents, donors of funds; in time, hopefully, every one will relax. All this is part of the student's education and his growing up.

Societies seeking accreditation should be asked to present a constitution and bylaws and a list of officers and to furnish information about purposes, affiliation, and officers (but not to list members by name; numbers are enough). Membership should be open to all students upon application; in the case of those societies with a specific political or religious orientation, it is up to their own membership to see that a group is not captured by those who essentially disagree with the stated purposes. If the student-activities council should have reason to believe that a society has concealed, misrepresented, or otherwise failed to disclose its purposes or affiliation, it may call for clarification. And what of failure to receive it? It is hoped that removal of accreditation will not be the penalty—although this is one of the risks of establishing responsible self-government. It is assumed that widespread publicity on the campus about the concealment will suffice to clear the air; in any event, the unwary will have been put on notice.

In view of the fact that all such student activities are in the family, the recording of such participation in student files is uncalled for: a good dean of students and his assistants will know these things, and that is enough. The danger of files is ease of access to them. And the revelation of names to noncollege persons or organizations or to any college personnel having no direct and legitimate interest in the matter is a breach of that confidentiality upon which the mutual trust of the academic community is founded.

Students are experimenting constantly with ideas and affiliations, sometimes of the most heterodox kind. Such identification or association—frequently of a highly transitory nature—should not be reported or forever remembered to affect the later life and career of a student.

A *sine qua non* for accreditation of a student society is *not* a required faculty adviser. Students apparently no longer want them and their wishes should be respected.

Similar observations are in order in the case of student publications—no advance approval of copy, no censorship, no faculty advisers; but open columns for dissenting opinions. In literary and humor magazines words and images not usually employed in polite discourse may crop up. The imagery may be poetic—and poetic license is very wide indeed. As for words and descriptions of bodily functions and sexual conduct (which occur in all the books the students are reading, from Chaucer and Shakespeare to Joyce and Genet), the courts have difficulty in defining obscenity or pornography. Why should college authorities try? Students sometimes will be shocking to gain attention or provoke: they are playing games. Relaxation on everyone's part is the word here, again.

Student newspapers run the danger of libel and obscenity laws and it is up to the editors to acquaint themselves of their legal rights and responsibilities. In the courts today, "libel" too is an elastic concept; not only public officials but also public personages (professional athletes, people in the entertainment world, men and women who associate themselves openly with causes) may be subjected widely to comment and criticism. The border line between criticism and malicious intent is hard to draw. One simply hopes that the freedom to write and publish given to students will sooner or later develop those responsibilities toward the accepted canons of good taste and fairness.

Some suggestions for academic due process for students already have been hinted at. It is being taken for granted that regulations for student conduct (and possible punishments) have been properly drawn up, discussed, and made available in handy form for all to read and learn. We have already spoken of student self-policing in certain matters with the creation of a student body to hear and pass judgment on those committing infractions.

There are major and minor student offenses. Action in the case of major offenses requires further discussion.

Today, when there is so much deep feeling about so many things on the part of students, it is not surprising that intemperate speech and conduct should occasionally appear. Regulations will say that assembly (demonstrations, picket lines, strikes, outdoor meetings) must be peaceable. They will also say that the legitimate or normal educational and institutional processes of the university must be honored. But what if students permit demonstrations to become riots?; or permit outdoor meetings to become so noisy that classroom activities and studying are seriously interfered with?; or permit sit-ins which prevent administrative officers from performing their business or recruiters, whether working for public or private organizations, from interviewing other students who are interested in learning of job opportunities or further training?

Granted that the strong emotions and unlawful conduct are due to conscience, it has already been said that regulations are drawn up to protect everyone's academic freedom—administrators, faculty, those students who happen to disagree with the demonstrators. Conscience is no defense for civil disobedience; the transgressor of society's rules for the maintenance of an orderly community must be brought to book. Otherwise, if each of us is to judge when he will be a good citizen and comply or when he will be a defiant one and not, law breaks down and anarchy results.

Those who are prepared to challenge law should be given a hearing with all due process safeguards. A hearing panel (always advisory) could be a standing or an *ad hoc* one, tripartite in composition with equal representation from administration, faculty, and students. Perhaps, because administration sometimes becomes too deeply involved in a dispute, it would be best for faculty representation to be elected from the faculty senate (or from the faculty members of a university council) and student representation elected from the above mentioned student-activity council (if there is one) or from the student-government organization, or from the students at large.

Rules of procedure for the conduct of a hearing should be drawn up and, if they work well the first time, incorporated into the regulations for student conduct already mentioned. The chairman of the panel preferably should be a faculty member.

Here are a few obvious safeguards as regards due process— and the protection of the reputations of all involved.

Once organized, the hearing panel should meet publicly; but it would be the counsel of wisdom to deny admission to the outside press and to radio and television.

Respondent and/or respondents should have the right to counsel, to confront witnesses, to cross-examine, to bring in witnesses. The charges against him or them should be in writing and should be explicit. Similarly the administration (presumably it is bringing charges of infraction) should have the same rights.

A transcript of the hearing should be made.

If students are found guilty as charged, the hearing panel should render a decision and recommend a punishment in each particular case, having in mind extenuating circumstances when offered by respondents or adduced from questioning.

Punishments will have a wide range: letter of admonition,

censure, disciplinary probation, suspension (one term a year), expulsion. Suspension and expulsion are serious; the hearing panel will know this—there is the draft; there is subsequent admission into professional and postgraduate schools if respondents are undergraduates; and character committees of many kinds for other students—and weigh its responsibilities carefully.

The findings and recommendations should go to the president of the university, for the charges have been brought (usually) by deans or deans of students and administrators have sat on the panel. He is likely—if he is a wise person—to review carefully findings and recommendations, scrutinizing each individual case and sometimes tempering justice with mercy and sometimes sentimentality with justice.

If the hearing is held with dispatch and the judgments rendered similarly; if its whole atmosphere has been demonstrably fair and dispassionate, the establishment and maintenance of order have been put to the test and have emerged successfully.

A final word: punishment having been ordered and accepted, it should end in the family. Keeping a permanent record of the nature of the offense (other than perhaps the judgment, whether "censure," "probation," etc.) threatens the future career and usefulness of a young man or woman who, upon impulse or strong feeling, disturbed the normal functioning of the community of which he was a part.

Whether we like it or not, students are becoming involved, some of them deeply, in matters that affect the national concern and the national security. Some are joining organizations—the extreme left, less frequently the extreme right—that advocate violence. Some are openly defying law: counseling others (high-school students, their classmates) not to register for the draft or to burn draft cards. To what extent should their mentors, deans of students, their teachers, disclose their knowledge of such activities and views of a similar nature voiced in the classroom? Some of their mentors in the university agree with the students, e.g., on the American involvement in Vietnam and the claim that an individual may reject a particular war and take steps to show his disapproval; but some do not. Whether agreeing or disagreeing, a good citizen, a thoughtful man, is confronted by the problem of disclosure when he is asked by an employer or prospective employer, or more particularly today by a governmental agency interested not in employment but in loyalty or, worse, conspiratorial acts, what has so-and-so done or said that may affect the national security?

The ACLU has taken the position—and the writer agrees; he helped in the formulation of the statement—that the teacher-student relation is a privileged one. The student, in the classroom, on the campus, has been encouraged, as part of the educational process, to probe, to share, to hypothesize, to think out loud, and to write what he thinks.

The student does not expect that what he has said or written in the classroom or in campus journals, or what he has said to teachers outside the classroom, will be reported beyond the walls of the college community. Violation of this confidentiality would end in distrust and in the sundering of that fine fabric of open give and take which is the basis of the sound relationship of student and teacher, of adult and youth.

To protect all concerned, it would be best if questions and answers from whatever source were handled in writing. Says the ACLU statement (published in 1961):

Ordinarily, questions relating to what the student has demonstrated as a student—for example, the ability to write in a certain way, to solve problems of a certain kind, to reason consistently, to direct personnel or other projects—pose no threat to educational privacy. But questions relating to the students loyalty or patriotism, his political or religious or moral or social beliefs and attitudes, his general outlook, his private life, may if answered jeopardize the teacher-student relationship. As a safeguard against the danger of putting the student in an unfavorable light with government representatives or employers of any category, simply as a result of the fact that some questions are answerable and others are not, teachers can preface each questionnaire with a brief *pro forma* statement that the academic policy to which they subscribe makes it inadvisable to answer certain types of questions. Once this academic policy becomes widespread, presumptive inferences about individual students will no longer be made by employers.

This, undoubtedly, is advice easy to give and hard to take. The lonely individual, battling with his ideas of justice and privilege on the one hand and his sense of duty on the other, is in serious difficulty. Unless faculty senates or other representative bodies take cognizance of the disclosure problem—as it affects not only teachers alone, but deans of students, other administrative officials, and other students too—the privacy of the student in this whole broad area still remains in an uncertain and insecure state. But this can be said: the unofficial presence on the campus of government representatives concerned with the national security, who are engaged frequently in fishing expeditions, is intolerable. Administrative officers, the president, deans, should insist that these persons first make their presence known to officials by identifying themselves and by indicating the specificity of their inquiries; and then get permission or not—bold counsel indeed! —to go about their business.

This last observation indicates how tentative and experimental many of the comments herein made are. If the reader has caught here and there a dogmatic note—certainty, even superiority, a presumed all-encompassing wisdom—the fault is in the imperfect writing and not in the writer. His long experience as a teacher, a friend of students, and a defender of student academic freedom has encouraged him to open up, explore, and offer his opinions on a number of troubled and troublesome problems. If others—college administrators, members of governing boards, government authorities, parents—will examine in a spirit of good will the questions raised here and some of the suggested answers proposed, many more of us than are doing today will be moving into and learning much from this terra incognita to which earlier reference has been made.

# V

# THE STRANGLEHOLD
# OF CENSORSHIP

## by ELMER RICE

Every social organism, from the simplest tribe to the most
complex industrial society, restricts by inherited tradition, arbitrary mandate, or legislative enactment, the freedom of the
individual. The prohibitions or taboos are bewilderingly
varied and comprehensive. They touch upon almost every
aspect of man's behavior and upon his relationship to his fel-
lows, to his social unit, and to nature. James G. Frazer, in *The
Golden Bough,* devotes a 400-page volume to a discussion of
taboos. Dress, food and drink, the bodily functions, the rites of
courtship, marriage, and burial are all subject to scrutiny and
regulation. Certain names or natural objects are regarded as
sacred or lethal and hence unmentionable or untouchable.
Ancient and primitive taboos are often hardy and persistent.
They survive in popular beliefs and in folk axioms and, for
example, in the dietary practices of modern Israel and India.
  Sometimes taboos do serve to protect the individual from

his own misguided behavior or to protect the community from antisocial acts. But in the main they are absurd, irrational, or contrived: the product of fear, superstition, ignorance, cruelty, or the self-interest of some dominant or powerful group. Whatever their nature or origin, the taboos may be so potent that their violation is likely to subject the individual to ostracism, exile, imprisonment, or even death.

As societies develop and social relationships grow more complex, the proscriptive emphasis tends to shift from the minutiae of personal behavior to conduct that has broader communal connotations. This is particularly true with respect to the multiplication of the means of communication. Where communication is limited to human speech, its regulation presents no great problem. But as supplemental means develop, the whole question of expression takes on ever-new aspects and its control becomes a matter of primary importance. One need not go all the way with Marshall McLuhan in his interpretation of history in terms of the emergence of new devices for communication: the written word, the printing press, and, very recently, the motion picture, radio, and television. But there can be no doubt that the rapid proliferation of the instruments of expression has profoundly affected the functioning of the social organism, the tempo of international relationships, and the habits and interests of the individual.

In general, it may be said that wherever books and newspapers are circulated, wherever plays, motion pictures, or telecasts are exhibited, there are restrictions upon freedom of expression. Contrary to popular belief, it is not the violation of sexual taboos that is most frequently suppressed or punished. What is chiefly condemned is the voicing of unorthodox political or religious opinions (and the two are often inseparable), particularly anything that questions the doctrines or policies of the existing governmental regime. The *Encyclopaedia Britannica* defines censorship as "an action taken by any governing authority to prevent the dissemination of false statements, inconvenient facts or displeasing opinions among the governed." This is a good enough working definition, though, as we shall see, effective suppression often goes beyond the limits of governmental action.

The more autocratic the regime the tighter is the stranglehold of censorship. Indeed, censorship is an inevitable concomitant of political or hierarchical absolutism. Freedom is not compatible with dictatorship, whether in a dynastic kingdom or a newly-emerged republic; whether in the communist states of Stalin, Mao, and Castro, or in the fascist states of Hitler, Mussolini, and Franco. In most of today's world lese majesty is still a punishable offense. The majority of mankind is not permitted to decide for itself what it wants to say and hear.

It is only in the political democracies of North America and Western Europe that the protection of the citizen against governmental infringement upon his personal liberty has been recognized not merely as a privilege but as a vested right. The principle of freedom of speech has become so well established that it is eulogized even by those who would place restrictions upon its application.

The struggle to entrench and buttress this right has been going on for centuries. One of its earliest and most eloquent defenders is John Milton. In 1643 the English Parliament enacted a law which provided that no book or other publication "shall from henceforth be printed or put to sale, unless the same be first approved or licensed by such person or persons as both or either of the said Houses shall appoint for the licensing of the same." Milton thereupon prepared a pamphlet titled *Areopagitica* which remains today, after three hundred years, perhaps the greatest statement for the case of free speech that has ever been written.

Pointing out the danger that lies in the arbitrary exercise of governmental power, Milton says:

> The state shall be my governors but not my critics; they may be mistaken in the choice of a licensor as easily as this licensor may be mistaken in an author . . . For though a licensor should happen to be judicious more

than ordinary . . . yet his very office and his commission enjoins him to let pass nothing but what is vulgarly received already.

Aware that censors tend to find acceptable only what is safely conventional and orthodox, Milton points out that we cannot know what is good unless we know what is evil, that we can recognize truth only by distinguishing it from falsehood. His words have a fine modern ring:

> Since therefore the knowledge and survey of vice is in this world so necessary to the constituting of human virtue, and the scanning of error to the confirmation of truth, how can we more safely, and with less danger, scout into the regions of sin and falsity than by reading all manner of tractates and hearing all manner of reason? And this is the benefit which may be had of books promiscuously read.

This was echoed by Justice Oliver Wendell Holmes when he wrote: "The best test of the truth is the power of the thought to get itself accepted in the competition of the market."

There has long been no licensing of books in England and no prepublication restraint upon what may be printed and circulated so that, strictly speaking, there is no censorship of books. However, there are statutes that do, in effect, act as restrictions upon complete freedom of expression. The English libel laws are so stringent that few publishers will run the risk of printing anything that might conceivably reflect unfavorably on any living person. For instance, in a book dealing with crime the author stated that a certain person had been convicted of rape. The person referred to brought an action for libel claiming that his character had been defamed because the offense for which he had been imprisoned was not rape but seduction. The publisher, fearing the outcome of a jury trial, made a substantial settlement out of court.

Moreover, there are laws against so-called obscenity. These have been frequently invoked: books have been confiscated and offenders subjected to fines or prison terms. In 1888 Henry Vizetelly, a highly respected publisher, was imprisoned for publishing the novels of Emile Zola. Old and ill, he died shortly after his release. But a recent case, equally celebrated, had a very different outcome. In 1960 the British Government instituted a criminal proceeding against Penguin Books Limited, publishers of D. H. Lawrence's famous novel, *Lady Chatterley's Lover,* which had previously been removed from the shelves of booksellers. In the course of the trial, which lasted for six days, the defense called to the witness stand a formidable company of authors, dons, editors, and clergymen who denied that the book was obscene and praised it for its literary, moral, and even religious quality. The result was a unanimous verdict of acquittal. (A detailed account of the trial may be found in *The Trial of Lady Chatterley,* edited by C. H. Rolph, Penguin, 1961.)

In America censorship has never taken the form of the licensing of books, though in colonial times certain restrictions upon publication were imposed by the Crown governors and (particularly upon religious works) by the Puritan settlers of New England who brought their dogmas and inhibitions with them: influences that survive in the words and actions of today's advocates of censorship—and not only in New England.

The press was also under strict surveillance and in 1734 John Peter Zenger, publisher of *The New York Journal,* was prosecuted for assailing the provincial government. Defying the instructions of the judge, the jury voted for acquittal. This was an important victory in the continuing struggle for freedom of the press and also for the establishment of an accused person's right to a jury trial.

Unlike England, the liberated colonies adopted a written constitution which defines the structure and the functions of the government of the United States of America. The Constitution was finally ratified in 1789 and amplified in 1791 by the adoption of ten amendments usually known as the Bill of Rights. The purpose of these amendments was to set forth the rights and immunities of the individual citizen and to prohibit their infringement by executive, legislative, or judicial action. The Fourteenth Amendment, which became part of the Constitution in 1868, provided that "no state shall make or enforce any law which shall abridge the privileges and immunities of citizens of the United States," thereby extending the application of the Bill of Rights to all the states of the Union.

The American Civil Liberties Union is a nonpolitical, nonpartisan, nonsectarian organization whose sole purpose is the protection and perpetuation of those rights and liberties guaranteed by the Bill of Rights to every American. It concerns itself not with debatable questions of doctrine, dogma, propriety, or morality, but only with safeguarding the rights of the individual within the structure of the law. These guaranteed rights include protection against search and seizure, against double jeopardy, against excessive bail, and against cruel and unusual punishments. They ensure the right to a jury trial, to the confrontation of an accused person by the witnesses against him, and to freedom of speech and of the press.

It is this free speech provision upon which the whole issue of censorship in the United States hinges. Set forth in the First Amendment it reads in full: "Congress shall make no law respecting an establishment of religion, or prohibiting the free exercise thereof; or abridging the freedom of speech, or of the press, or the right of the people peaceably to assemble, and to petition the government for a redress of grievances."

This clear and unequivocal language would seem to preclude any form of censorship or control of expression. Yet there are many factors that militate against the strict application of the First Amendment. These include the overlapping jurisdictions of national, state, and sometimes municipal authorities; the conflicts among the executive, legislative, and judicial branches of the government; the problems involved in dealing with new forms of communication; the virtually monopolistic control of communications media; and the influences and pressures exerted by commercial advertisers and by innumerable groups organized for the purpose of furthering some special interest. Hence the situation is constantly changing and the whole subject is beset with complexities.

Though the First Amendment has effectually prevented the setting up of any form of licensing or other prior restraint, the federal government has used its authority to restrict the circulation of printed and graphic material. Acting under its power to control imports, Congress in 1842 forbade the entry into this country of obscene pictures; this proscription was extended in 1890 to obscene literature. Similarly, and apparently on the theory that the use of the mails is a "privilege" and not a right, the Comstock Act of 1873 (so named in honor of the militant vice crusader, Anthony Comstock) barred objectionable material from the mails.

The establishment of these restrictions certainly seems contrary to the spirit of the First Amendment, particularly when one considers that their execution is entrusted to civil service employees or political appointees whose qualifications for the role of censor are, to say the least, dubious. Furthermore, these officials act arbitrarily under procedures that make no provision for a fair trial thus violating the due process of law guarantees of the Bill of Rights. Consequently, the subject has given rise to considerable litigation and to agitation for the modification or revocation of the unwarranted powers. Whenever it has been possible to carry a case to the higher courts, the judicial tendency has been to limit the censorial activities of administrative officers. The customs ban on *Ulysses, Lady Chatterley's Lover,* and *Tropic of Cancer* were overruled; and the Post Office Department was debarred from denying second-class mailing privileges (and thereby effectually preventing the circulation) of the periodicals *Esquire* and *Sunshine and Health* (a nudist publication). Recently, attempts to interfere with the delivery of communist literature mailed abroad have been held valid by the Supreme Court.

A far wider area of governmental restraint is found in the statutes, enacted by almost every state and by many municipalities, which make the publication or distribution of obscene material a crime punishable by fine or imprisonment. These laws have given rise to endless debate and litigation for it seems that there is no generally accepted definition of obscenity and no precise criterion for its recognition. To use such terms as lewd, lascivious, licentious, or even the Supreme Court definition (see below), is merely to follow a chain of adjectives which leads back to the beginning.

The courts have dealt with this question repeatedly. The resultant decisions and opinions have been confusing and often contradictory. In 1868 Lord Chief Justice Cockburn of England laid down this dictum (known as the Hicklin rule): "I think the test of obscenity is this, whether the tendency of the matter charged as obscenity is to deprave and corrupt those whose minds are open to such immoral influences, and into whose hands a publication of this sort may fall."

The Hicklin rule had wide judicial acceptance both in England and the United States. But it came gradually to be questioned and in 1913 Judge Learned Hand of the United States District Court said of it: "I hope it is not improper for me to say that the rule as laid down, however consonant it may be with Victorian morals, does not seem to me to answer to the morality and understanding of the present time."

Subsequent decisions cast further doubt upon the validity of the Hicklin rule. In 1949 Federal Judge Curtis Bok said:

The full weight of the legislative prohibition dangles from the word "obscene" and its synonyms. Nowhere are these words defined; nowhere is the danger to be expected of them stated; nowhere is a standard of judgment set forth. I assume that "obscenity" is expected to have a familiar and inherent meaning, both as to what it is and as to what it does. It is my purpose to show that it has no such inherent meaning; that different meanings given to it at different times are not constant, either historically or legally; and that it is not constitutionally indictable unless it takes the form of sexual impurity, i.e. "dirt for dirt's sake," and can be traced to actual criminal behavior, either actual or demonstrably imminent.

In general, this states the position taken by the American Civil Liberties Union with respect to prosecutions for obscenity. It reaffirms the so-called clear and present danger rule as enunciated by Justices Brandeis and Holmes in *Whitney* v. *California,* 1927: "To justify suppression of free speech there must be reasonable ground to fear that serious evil will result if free speech is practised. There must be reasonable ground to believe that the danger apprehended is imminent. There must be reasonable ground to believe that the evil to be prevented is a serious one." In 1919, in *Schenck* v. *U.S.,* the whole Court had declared: "The question in every case is whether the words used are used in such circumstances and are of such a nature as to create a clear and present danger that they will bring about the substantive evils that the state has a right to prevent."

*Banned Books* by Anne Lyon Haight (Bowker, 1955) contains a long (but by no means exhaustive) list of books that have been subject to suppression or attempted suppression. It includes many of the classics of world literature as well as important contemporary works. A random sampling comprises Ovid's *Ars Amatoria;* Aristophanes' *Lysistrata;* Voltaire's *Candide;* De Sade's *Justine;* Balzac's *Droll Stories;* Havelock Ellis' *Studies in the Psychology of Sex;* Theodore Dreiser's *An American Tragedy;* D. H. Lawrence's *Lady Chatterley's Lover;* Sinclair Lewis' *Elmer Gantry;* Lillian Smith's *Strange Fruit;* Ernest Hemingway's *The Sun Also Rises;* Erskine Caldwell's *God's Little Acre;* and James Farrell's *Studs Lonigan.*

All these books have been banned or prosecuted by customs and post-office officials, district attorneys, and local police authorities and by such self-appointed guardians of the public's morals as the New York Society for the Suppression of Vice and the Boston Watch and Ward Society. The outcome of these censorial actions has been variable and unpredictable, depending upon the educational background, psychological conditioning, and reasoning power of civil servants and jurors. Nor has there been any unanimity or consistency in the decisions of the courts. Books that are adjudged obscene in one state are absolved in another. Appellate courts sometimes affirm, sometimes reverse (and often by a divided vote) convictions obtained in the courts below.

If the clear and present danger rule were the sole criterion, there could perhaps never be a successful prosecution of a book. For it is almost impossible to establish a direct causal relationship between what an individual reads and his commission or probable commission of criminal or antisocial acts. Criminologists and psychologists have varying views on this subject, but the consensus seems to be that the study of human behavior is not sufficiently advanced to permit sound judgments of the effect of cultural stimuli upon conduct.

The position of the American Civil Liberties Union is clearly stated in its policy guide:

> The Constitutional protection of freedom of speech and of the press is guaranteed by the First Amendment to all expression. The ACLU believes that only those utterances that create a clear and present danger to society can be restricted.
> Because there is no definite proof that "obscene" material does expose the community to such a clear and present danger, laws which limit freedom of speech or of the press on grounds of obscenity are unjustified, and "obscenity" as a legal classification is without basis.

But this by no means disposes of the matter. There are many civil libertarians who believe that, while no publication of literary value should be subject to prosecution, some limit should be placed upon the circulation of "hard core pornography," or what Judge Bok has called "dirt for dirt's sake." But when one examines the implications of this position one finds that these terms are no easier to define than is obscenity itself. These are epithets, not descriptive phrases that can be objectively applied to specific material. Again it comes down to the psychological quirks of the individual who makes the judgment.

The question of the applicability of the First Amendment to

allegedly obscene material was long bypassed by the Supreme Court. In 1957, however, it faced the issue squarely in the historic *Roth* v. *United States* decision.[1] Though a minority took the ACLU view that all forms of expression are equally protected, the majority held that material without "redeeming social importance" does not come within the constitutional guarantee. It did not state how this determination was to be arrived at. But the Court went on to declare that the test of obscenity was "whether to the average person, applying community standards, the dominant theme of the material taken as a whole appeals to prurient interest, i.e. a shameful or morbid interest in nudity, sex or excretion." It narrowed this definition somewhat in later decisions by saying that the material must be "patently offensive" and that the community standards should be national rather than local, thereby limiting the likelihood of convictions by provincial juries.

Again the decision bristles with terms and standards not susceptible of precise definition, leaving the determination in a particular case to the subjectivity of the juror or the judge. The Supreme Court in 1965 added to the general confusion by upholding the conviction of Ralph Ginzburg on an obscenity charge. Ginzburg was the publisher of a periodical and several books which a lower court found obscene. He was fined $28,000 and sentenced to five years' imprisonment, a punishment of unusual severity. The Supreme Court's 5 to 4 decision was predicated upon the extraordinary premise that though the material in itself might not have been adjudged obscene, it became so by the manner in which it was exploited and advertised. Said Mr. Justice Brennan: "The 'leer of the sensualist' . . . permeates the advertising for the three publications. The deliberate representation of . . . the publications as erotically arousing . . . stimulated the reader to accept them as prurient; he looks for titillation, not for saving intellectual content." In dissent Mr. Justice Black said: "The fact

[1] Samuel Roth, a book dealer in New York, had been convicted on four counts of mailing obscene circulars, advertisements, and a book in violation of a Federal obscenity statute. [*Editor*]

is that Ginzburg . . . is now finally and authoritatively condemned to serve five years in prison for distributing printed
matter about sex, which neither Ginzburg nor anyone else
could possibly have known to be criminal." [2]

Though ambiguous and often contradictory decisions leave
the door open for prosecutions under obscenity laws, in actual
practice there has been a marked tendency to broaden the
protections of the First Amendment. In 1946 Doubleday, the
publisher of Edmund Wilson's *Memoirs of Hecate County*,
was convicted on an obscenity charge in the New York County
court of special sessions. The conviction was upheld on successive appeals and finally, by a 4 to 4 vote, in the United
States Supreme Court. There is little likelihood that this book,
if it were published today, would even attract the notice of a
public prosecutor or vice crusader or that, if it were brought
into a court, a jury or judge would find it guilty. In case after
case the courts have cleared books long proscribed; for example, *Tropic of Cancer*, *Lady Chatterley's Lover*, and *Fanny
Hill* (the last at the same session of the Supreme Court which
upheld the conviction of Ginzburg).

The judicial movement in the direction of liberalization is
part of a general trend toward permissiveness. Courts do not
operate in a vacuum; and while it may not be true, as Mr.
Dooley said, that the Supreme Court follows the election re-
turns, judges are susceptible to public pressure and are influenced by the *mores* or what the Supreme Court, in the Roth

[2] Two years after the Ginzburg conviction, the Supreme Court enumerated three possible grounds which might justify the suppression of a
work. In *Redrup* v. *New York* the high court reversed three separate
obscenity convictions involving two paperback books and eleven magazines. The Court's statement in the Redrup case may constitute a new
definition of legal censorship: "In none of the cases was there a claim that
the statute in question reflected a specific and limited state concern for
juveniles. . . . In none was there any suggestion of an assault upon
individual privacy by publication in a manner so obtrusive as to make
it impossible for an unwilling individual to avoid exposure to it. . . .
And in none was there evidence of the sort of 'pandering' which the
Court found significant in *Ginzburg* v. *United States*."

In 1968, Ginzburg was still free while awaiting final court determination of his further appeal of the sentence. [*Editor*]

case, called "community standards." These standards often control social behavior far more effectively than do prohibitory statutes. There is no law against picking one's nose, belching, or breaking wind in public, yet most people are deterred from such acts by fear of popular disapproval. But the *mores* are neither consistent nor persistent. The limits of propriety are often ill-defined and extensible.

In the twentieth century, and particularly since the end of World War II, there have been extraordinary changes in many areas of behavior. At the turn of the century no "respectable" woman drank, smoked, or dined alone in public; only a sophisticated few used cosmetics. Skirts that once trailed the ground now reveal the thighs; bathing attire has shrunk to the vanishing point. Premarital intercourse, venereal disease, homosexuality, abortion, and contraception are freely and frankly discussed not only in newspapers and magazines, which once shunned any reference to these subjects, but on radio and television programs.

This outspokenness is reflected in contemporary literature (to use that word in its broadest sense). For literature does not create the *mores;* it merely expresses them and gives them articulate form. It is not surprising, therefore, to find in books an increasing preoccupation with subjects that occupy public attention and, as a corollary, with graphic, explicit descriptions of physiological behavior. At the same time the "four-letter" words (not more than a dozen in all), for so long strictly taboo, are now used so freely in writing and in speech that their shock value has almost vanished.

Whether this new frankness is a therapeutic release from unhealthy inhibitions and repressions, a needed liberation from Victorian prudery or hypocrisy, or, as others contend, a deplorable lowering of socially desirable standards of decency and evidence of a decay of the community's moral fiber, is a question to which no satisfactory answer can be given. Psychologists, educators, sociologists, ministers of religion debate vehemently and endlessly only to come up with irreconcilable conclusions. As is so often the case when moral issues are involved, the opinions are usually based upon psychological conditioning rather than upon demonstrable evidence. Therefore, the civil libertarian, though he may find this or that example of literary expression personally distasteful, believes that the essence of democracy is freedom of choice and that the determination of what is fitting and proper should be left to the judgment of the individual and not to the arbitrary decision of a censor.

Many of those who accept the principle that every adult should have complete freedom of choice believe that a different policy should be adopted with respect to children. Children, they contend, are not capable of making valid judgments and should therefore be protected by law against the possible harmful consequences of their exposure not only to material that is obscene, but to material that stresses violence and sadism. In opposition to this view is the belief that the supervision of children's reading (or viewing) is a parental and not a governmental function and, further, that it is almost impossible to limit what is available to children without also putting restrictions upon adults. But the strongest argument is that there is no convincing body of evidence that a causal relationship exists between a child's reading and his behavior; or, specifically, that exposure to certain types of material leads to the commission of antisocial or destructive acts. While some competent students of the question believe that the connection does exist, there are many who disagree, some holding that juvenile delinquents tend to be nonreaders, others affirming that a child's vicarious participation in violence is a healthy outlet for his aggressiveness. Perhaps most qualified observers are inclined, in the absence of clear-cut proof, to withhold their judgment. In view of all this the ACLU has adopted the following policy: "Until it is shown that the circulation of crime comic books constitutes a clear and present danger with respect to the occurrence, or continuance, of juvenile delinquency, there is no justification for curtailing a basic right guaranteed by the Constitution."

The theater is another area in which the censor and the

would-be censor have always been active, particularly when organized religion plays an important part in the councils of state. Though the drama is religious in origin, the evangelical church has always looked upon the theater with disfavor. The playhouse is regarded as the abode of Satan: a hotbed of licentiousness and immorality. Some sects forbid playgoing altogether.

In England, under Cromwell, the theaters were shut down entirely. Though they reopened after the Restoration, a censorship of the stage was subsequently established by the setting up of a licensing system for plays. All plays must be submitted prior to production to the Lord Chamberlain who has the power to prohibit the acting of an entire play or any portion of it whenever "he shall be of the opinion that it is fitting for the preservation of good manners, decorum or of the public peace so to do." This sumptuary enactment has resulted in the banning of Sophocles' *Oedipus;* Shelley's *The Cenci;* Ibsen's *Ghosts;* Wilde's *Salome;* Shaw's *Shewing Up of Blanco Posnet;* Granville-Barker's *Waste;* O'Neill's *Desire Under the Elms;* and Connelly's *The Green Pastures*—to name only a few of the important plays that have been denied a license as recently as 1931 by the Lord Chamberlain.[3]

Repeated attempts, initiated by prominent individuals in all walks of life, have been made to abolish this antiquated institution. There have been petitions to Parliament, protest meetings, and public hearings. But the censorship continues. However, means have been found to circumvent it. When a play is denied a license, the producer simply organizes a "theater club," membership in which (available to practically anyone) enables one to buy tickets for the play. Since the Lord Chamberlain's authority is limited to the regulation of "public" performances, this ludicrously transparent device makes possible the production of almost any play (though sometimes in an out-of-the-way theater).

[3] The ban applies only to public theaters; the plays could always be given in "private" clubs, which were easily accessible to the public. [*Editor*]

In the United States, too, the theater has always been the whipping boy of the morally censorious. Periodically there are outcries against the excesses of the drama and demands for repressive measures. Some years ago a well-known "liberal" clergyman declared in a sermon that the New York stage was given over to filth. When asked to supply a bill of particulars, he admitted that he had not seen a single current play, but had relied upon the report of one of his female parishioners.

But no licensing system or other form of regulation has ever been established. Repeated efforts have been made to set up a stage censorship in New York State (since New York City is the chief center of theatrical activity) but the combined efforts of the Actors Equity Association, the Dramatists Guild, and the League of New York Theatres have always resulted in the defeat of the proposed legislation. The New York obscenity law is applicable to the drama and if a play is adjudged obscene, the license of the theater may be suspended for one year but only *after* a jury trial and a conviction. Various attempts to establish "play juries" of prominent citizens—a disguised form of censorship—have been successfully opposed by the theatrical profession aided by free speech advocates.

Since it is chiefly in large cities that plays are professionally performed, it is not surprising to find that censorship was hard at work in various municipalities although it happily is now dying out. Among the cities in which there had been frequent interference with the performance of plays are Providence, Chicago, Boston, and New York. In these communities the mayor, police commissioner, or other public official arrogates to himself, usually illegally, the power to censor plays.

Boston has long had in effect a *de facto* licensing system under which a political functionary examines play scripts and either orders expurgations or forbids performance. Plays that have been completely banned in Boston include O'Casey's *Within the Gates* (sacrilege); Hellman's *The Children's Hour* (lesbianism); Odets' *Waiting for Lefty* (political radicalism); Anderson's and Hickerson's *Gods of the Lightning* (the Sacco-

Vanzetti case; a sensitive subject in Boston); O'Neill's *Desire Under the Elms* and *Strange Interlude* (sexual immorality). When the last-named play was interdicted, the producers gave performances in a large tent just outside the city limits to which the eager Bostonians flocked.

In New York during the 1930's Mayor LaGuardia, in general a man of liberal tendencies, conducted a sort of crusade against the theater by authorizing the Commissioner of Licenses to revoke or threaten to revoke the licenses of playhouses in which objectionable performances were given. This was a wholly illegal procedure, for the granting of theater licenses is an administrative function unrelated to scrutiny of the plays performed. Presumably LaGuardia's chief targets were the burlesque shows and the plays of Mae West; but, as was to be expected, the Commissioner soon set himself up as an arbiter of what might fittingly be seen on the stage.

Among the plays that over the years have been subjected to prosecution or other forms of interference in New York are Ibsen's *Ghosts;* Shaw's *Mrs. Warren's Profession;* Brieux's *Damaged Goods;* Asch's *The God of Vengeance;* Gantillon's *Maya;* Bourdet's *The Captive;* Sartre's *The Respectful Prostitute.* Most of these plays were earnest discussions of vital social problems. A New York State law, enacted at the behest of the Catholic hierarchy, which forbids the representation of any member of the Trinity upon the stage, has seldom, if ever, been invoked. Indeed, Connelly's *The Green Pastures,* in which De Lawd plays a leading part, was highly commended by the clergy (though some prominent Negroes thought the play should be withdrawn, because it seemed to them that it presented the religious faith of the Negro in a patronizing and rather ridiculous light).

With plays, as with books, the likelihood of censorship diminishes as the range of the permissible widens. Sixty years ago the posthumous production of Clyde Fitch's play, *The City,* caused a sensation because the words "God damn" were used for the first time upon a New York stage. Today the general relaxation of taboos in language and in behavior is reflected in the theater. As long as no one is compelled to attend a performance that he finds distasteful the fixing of the limits of propriety may well be left to the operation of the *mores*.

In contrast to the rigidly controlled press of totalitarian governments, newspapers and magazines in the United States have been almost entirely free from censorship. They sometimes run afoul of post-office regulations or obscenity laws, but recourse may be had to the courts often with favorable results. There is, however, no licensing system and no prepublication scrutiny. The shrinkage in the number of newspapers, the tendency toward monopolization of ownership, and the syndication of content undoubtedly lead to standardization and conformity, as does a catering to the predilections of large advertisers upon whom the press is economically dependent. But there are still some large-circulation newspapers that maintain their independence, as well as innumerable publications that appeal to almost any taste or shade of opinion, thus providing the diversity of expression which is the essence of free speech.

Until the twentieth century the existent vehicles of expression—books, plays, periodicals—were read and seen only by a minority of the population. Illiteracy, indifference, and inadequate circulation facilities put limits upon distribution. But the recently invented media of mass communication have created an audience that includes practically everybody except newborn infants, regardless of occupation, social status, education, or intelligence. As Marshall McLuhan and others have pointed out, these new media have radically altered the shape of society and have given rise to problems that could not have been foreseen by John Milton or even by the authors of the Bill of Rights.

It was not long after its first public exhibition that the motion picture was subjected to governmental control. Indeed, the motion picture is the only medium of expression that has ever been hampered by precensorship. New York and six or seven other states set up censorship boards which had arbitrary power to expurgate a picture or to ban it in its entirety.

Since nearly all the states in the Union accepted the judgment of the New York board, denial of a license by New York amounted, in effect, to complete suppression.

Civil libertarians, of course, contended from the very beginning that the establishment of the censorship boards violated the free speech guarantees of the Bill of Rights. But when a test case was carried to the United States Supreme Court in 1915, the Court ruled that motion pictures were not essentially a medium for the communication of ideas and not so much an art as an industry. This rule was the law of the land for more than thirty-five years, during which the power of the censor, though repeatedly challenged, remained practically unimpaired. In 1952, however, the Court, in a unanimous decision, admitted motion pictures to the protection of the First Amendment by reversing a New York decision which had banned a picture called *The Miracle* under a state statute which prohibited the exhibition of sacrilegious material. The Court, applying the due process of law test, voided the statute upon the ground of vagueness (as it had done in 1948 with respect to a New York statute forbidding the publication of material made up principally of pictures or stories of "deeds of bloodshed, lust or crime").

In deciding *The Miracle* case the Court left open the question "whether a state may censor motion pictures under a clearly drawn statute designed and applied to prevent the showing of obscene films." In spite of this reservation the Court's decisions, in this case and in other cases overruling the banning of films, have resulted in either the abolition of the censorship boards or in a drastic reduction in their effectiveness. The Court has shown a tendency, too, to scrutinize strictly statutes that seek to set up censorship; it has held that such laws must put the burden of proof upon the would-be censor and that they must provide for a swift and open trial with the usual due process safeguards prescribed for any criminal action. So that while there are still sporadic attempts, sometimes successful, on the part of municipal authorities to suppress this or that film, such actions are usually frowned upon by the courts, and it may be said that precensorship of motion pictures in the United States has been almost entirely abolished.[4]

The question of whether or not some form of regulation is necessary for the protection of children arises again with respect to motion pictures. Here, too, there is a wide difference of opinion. Many persons who oppose censorship in general advocate the adoption of a system of classification whereby films would be put into categories determined by their suitability for children. In fact, this proposal is a sort of rear guard action of the emasculated New York State censorship board. Reasons for opposing the plan are set forth in the policy guide of the American Civil Liberties Union:

> Film classification is a form of prior censorship and thus violates the First Amendment. Although certain films are thought by some members of the community to be unsuitable for children, it is up to parents, not governmental agencies, to decide what films their children should see. . . . The divergent views of parents on this subject are so numerous that it would be impossible for any official authority to formulate a consistently wise policy that could be applied to all children. In addition, the censorship bureaucracy required to operate a classification system would encourage the growth of a vested interest in the suppression of expression, while the members of such a bureaucracy would necessarily be guided by individual and secret standards of judgment.[5]

[4] Today only Maryland has a censorship statute and it operates only within strict procedural limitations. The only two cities with censorship boards still functioning are Chicago and Dallas and both are being challenged. [*Editor*]

[5] Film-classification boards in Dallas and Chicago have been declared invalid in court decisions, either on grounds of vagueness or the broad scope of the ordinances. However, the U.S. Supreme Court has upheld the right of the state to regulate the sale of materials to young people. In 1968 the Court upheld a New York statute that forbids the sale of material defined as obscene to minors under seventeen. [*Editor*]

Even further reaching in their scope and influence than motion pictures are those relatively new media of communication, radio and television. Radio has been in general use only since World War I and television only since World War II. Yet the growth of both has been so rapid that broadcasting today has become the most widespread and perhaps the most influential means of human expression. Though radio is entirely auditory and television is largely visual, they constitute, from the civil liberties point of view, a single medium, and this interpretation gives rise to many complex free speech issues.

In almost every country broadcasting is either operated directly by the government or by some quasi-governmental agency like the British Broadcasting Company. (Though recently privately owned, commercial broadcasters have come into strong competition with the BBC.) Under any form of governmental operation, censorship necessarily exists since the governmental agency has the arbitrary power to determine what may or may not be seen and heard.

In the United States broadcasting has always been conducted as a private enterprise (except, perhaps, for a few municipally operated stations). Unlike the motion-picture industry the broadcasters have never been subject to prior censorship. In fact, the Federal Communications Act specifically prohibits the establishment of such a censorship. However, since radio wave lengths and television channels are limited in number, it was necessary to provide some system of allocation and control, particularly since what is involved is the free use by private entrepreneurs of the air waves, which, like the highways and waterways, rightfully belong to all the people.

Accordingly, the Act created the Federal Communications Commission, which has the power to grant licenses to radio and TV stations. Though the Commission has no control over program material as such, it does have the right to refuse the renewal of a license to a station whose overall programming does not, in the opinion of the FCC, serve the "public interest, convenience and necessity." Such abuse of the license is not easy to establish and denials of renewal have been relatively few.

But the mere absence of official censorship does not ensure that complete freedom from restriction which is the concern of the civil libertarian. Various factors tend to limit not only diversity in programming but the content of the programs themselves. As in the newspaper field, the concontration of ownership in a few hands tends to make for uniformity and for a resistance to unorthodoxy.

Even greater is the restrictive influence of the advertisers upon whose sponsorship of programs the broadcasters depend for their very handsome profits. Almost always, the sponsor has control over the content of the program and since he is primarily interested in selling something rather than in provocative discussion or unconventional attitudes, he is likely to insist upon the presentation of what he thinks will attract the largest number of potential customers. This inevitably makes for standardization and banality and militates against diversity.

Also restrictive is the policy of "self-regulation" adopted by the broadcasting industry and by the motion-picture industry as well. Both the National Association of Broadcasters and the Motion Picture Association of America have, from time to time, issued codes which specify what subjects are not permissible on the television and motion-picture screens. Both codes cover a wide range of taboos: attacks on religions and religious faiths; narcotic addiction, except as a vicious habit; suicide and divorce as solutions of human problems; sex crimes and abnormalities; ridicule of racial or nationality types; profanity, obscenity, smut, and vulgarity; and many other subjects.

In the motion-picture field it was the practice of producers to submit scenarios to the Production Code Administration, which ordered the deletion of material that was considered violative of the code. If a completed picture passed the scrutiny of the Administration, it was granted a seal of approval. This seal was almost essential to the successful exploitation of a picture, for without it, bookings were often refused by exhibitors who feared prosecution under state statutes. But as the number of independent producers increased the code began to lose some of its efficacy. Changes in community standards coupled with the profitable exhibition of some pictures that were denied the seal resulted in liberalization of the code and its application. To give only one example, the 1930 code states flatly that "sex perversion or any inference of it is forbidden." But the 1966 version of this proscription is: "Restraint and care shall be exercised in presentations dealing with sex aberrations." [6]

The television code was first issued in 1952 by the National Association of Broadcasters, which authorized the Television Board "to enact, amend and promulgate standards of practice or codes for its television members and to establish such methods to secure observance thereof, as it may deem advisable." But, as in all other forms of expression, the range of permissibility has been greatly widened and there is a growing tendency to ignore or evade the rigid restrictions of the code.

It is often argued that self-regulation is not censorship but is merely an exercise of the motion-picture or television producer's right to decide what he shall offer to the public. There can, of course, be no doubt that the independent publisher or theatrical producer has every right to reject a book or a play that does not happen to suit his taste even though his decision may be the product of ignorance or cowardice. But a very different situation exists in the monopolistic mass communication fields, where the adoption of an industry-wide code with sanctions is tantamount to arbitrary restraint.

Shortly after World War II, another limitation upon freedom of expression in the motion-picture and broadcasting fields took the form of blacklisting: the denial of employment

[6] Although there are no written sanctions for violation of the Code, the ACLU still opposes it because it imposes a prior restraint on the entire industry which may discourage or prevent artists from treating certain themes or cause alterations during production to satisfy Code standards, thus stifling free expression. [Editor]

to certain writers (as well as actors and directors), not because of what they wrote, but because of their alleged political affiliations. This deplorable practice was a byproduct of the anticommunist uproar fomented by the late Senator McCarthy. An organization calling itself American Business Consultants, operated by former Federal Bureau of Investigation agents, issued newsletters and eventually a paperback book, called *Red Channels,* which listed the names of individuals in the entertainment world who were reputedly Communists or Communist sympathizers. Offered as proof was a listing of the "subversive" organizations with which each person allegedly had had some connection.

Soon after the publication of *Red Channels,* writers and performers listed in it (and others who had availed themselves of the protection from self-incrimination, provided by the Fifth Amendment to the Constitution) began to find that they could no longer get jobs in motion pictures or on the air. This deplorable practice soon became widespread. It was characterized by the ACLU as "a serious blow to the public interest because it infringes upon the author's freedom of expression" and also because "it denies the public its right to see or hear artists or their products for totally irrelevant considerations."

Since no producer was obliged to employ any specific person unless he chose to do so, it was almost impossible for the opponents of blacklisting to combat it. Though *Red Channels* was facetiously known in broadcasting circles as "the bible of Madison Avenue," industry spokesmen denied the existence of a blanket policy. Indeed, it is likely that no formal agreement to blacklist was ever made but that the policymakers acted concertedly on the basis of a tacit understanding. The blacklist, in effect for some years, began to diminish when the United States Senate's disciplinary action against Senator McCarthy and his death shortly afterward brought about an abatement of the anticommunist hysteria. Meanwhile, the blacklist had injured the reputation and impaired the livelihood of many well-known motion-picture and broadcasting personalities. One of them, John Henry Faulk, brought a libel suit against his accusers and was eventually awarded $3,500,-000 in damages.[7] Though sporadic examples of blacklisting still occur, it no longer seems a major problem. However, its practice has put a stain of dishonor on the mass media; nor is there any certainty that in similar circumstances it would not recur.

Because the number of available outlets and prime reception time are limited and because programmatic material caters mainly to the requirements of the commercial sponsors, there is, on the air, a lack of that complete diversity of expression which is the desideratum of the free speech advocate who does not seek to exercise control over the nature or content of programs but merely to extend their scope and variety. Thus the civil libertarian favors the licensing, on a nonmonopolistic basis, of more channels in the Ultra High Frequency spectrum; unsponsored pay television; Community Antenna Television, on a tentative and experimental basis; and an increase in the number of noncommercial educational stations, not only for the teaching of academic subjects but for the broadcasting of material that appeals to limited audiences. Though lack of diversity does not in itself constitute censorship, it does act as a restraining force upon unhampered free speech.

No study of censorship would be complete without consideration of the role played by private organizations in the suppression or attempted suppression of freedom of expression. These organizations are innumerable, for they include legislative lobbies for various economic and political interests; professional associations of every sort; religious, ethnic, racial, and educational aggregations. Collectively, they are often referred to as pressure groups because of their influence upon legislation, law enforcement, and the activities of the media of communication.

[7] The Appellate Division of the New York Supreme Court cut the award to $550,000 in November, 1963. In his book *Fear on Trial*, Faulk mentioned that collection might be difficult because the defendants' estates were not as large as the courts had thought. [*Editor*]

Many, perhaps most, of these groups were created for the commendable purpose of protecting and furthering the rights and interests of their membership whether it consists of industrial workers, lawyers, doctors, actors, Catholics, Jews, Negroes, or war veterans. It is quite proper for them to advocate or to decry whatever seems to them helpful or harmful to the welfare or integrity of the particular group or to the principles to which it is committed. Indeed, their right to speak and to assemble is guaranteed by the First Amendment and is vigorously defended by civil libertarians, notably the American Civil Liberties Union, regardless of approval or disapproval of the point of view involved.

In the area of communication, it is not surprising that these pressure groups often seek to limit or prohibit the dissemination of cultural material which they regard as inimical to their special interests. Hence, conflict often arises between the right of the minority group—and it is necessarily always a minority group—to give overt expression to its opposition and the right of the majority (or even of another minority) to see and to hear whatever it chooses to. The balance is a delicate one and not easy to maintain.

The ACLU policy statement on private pressure groups, after declaring that "the judgment of any particular group must not be allowed to usurp the freedom of choice of the whole community," goes on to say: "The Union makes a clear distinction between the right of all organizations to express their opinions, and actions that deny those who do not agree with these opinions an opportunity to examine for themselves the book or film in question."

Pressure is of various sorts and of varying degrees of effectiveness. Sometimes it is trivial and even borders upon the ludicrous. An apple-growers' association demanded the elimination of a speech in a play in which a character remarked that the apple he was eating had been sprayed with arsenic. A hotel employees' union picketed a theater presenting a play in which a comic chambermaid was depicted as performing her duties in a perfunctory manner. The American Bar Associ-

ation requested changes in a play which allegedly showed
lawyers in an unfavorable light. The play was Arthur Miller's
*The Crucible;* the lawyers portrayed were those involved in
the seventeenth-century Salem witch trials. On the air, pressure from Negro organizations resulted in the substitution of
"children" for "darkies" in the lyric of that old favorite, "My
Old Kentucky Home."

But there are many powerful groups whose pressures do
seriously affect freedom of communication. Among them are
such organizations as the Catholic Legion of Decency, the
Jewish Anti-Defamation League, the American Legion, and
the Daughters of the American Revolution. For example, in the
1950's a periodical, *The Nation,* was banned from the New
York public schools because of its publication of anti-Catholic
articles (the ban has since been rescinded), and in Oklahoma
a librarian who subscribed to it was dismissed when an American Legion post denounced her as a subversive. In the North-
west utility companies have been charged with attempting to
prevent schools from using textbooks that advocate public
ownership.

These are outward evidences of a troublesome situation.
Obviously, no school or library could afford to purchase every
book that is published even if it were desirable to do so.
Therefore, choices must be made and it is quite likely that the
librarian, especially in small communities, will defer to the
pressures of the special interest groups and confine his pur-
chases to books that are not regarded as offensive.

Numerous pressure groups, mainly ethnic, political, and religious, mount open or behind-the-scenes campaigns to remove
from public view what they regard as offensive. Negro and
Jewish groups attempt to suppress the portrayal of what they
call racial stereotypes or indeed to anything that offends their
sensibilities. *Amos 'n' Andy, Beulah, The Birth of a Nation,
Uncle Tom's Cabin,* and minstrel shows have been attacked and
sometimes suppressed. Jewish organizations have tried to prevent a telecast of *The Merchant of Venice.* Margaret Webster,
a well-known actress and director, was forced to drop this

play from her repertory when Jewish campus groups threatened to boycott her entire program. Jewish leaders have even advocated the removal from the shelves of school libraries of any books that disparage Jews. Veterans' organizations and patriotic societies take repressive action not only against material that does not measure up to their standards of "Americanism" but against nonpolitical works that are written or performed by individuals whom they regard as "subversive." Scripts portraying ministers of religion are often submitted to church authorities for approval (or revision) before they are filmed or broadcast. Radio and television sponsors are particularly careful about excising anything that might alienate the potential purchasers of their products. Since there is no way of knowing what might have been written or shown if these pressures did not exist, their exact effect cannot be measured, but there can be no doubt that, in the aggregate, the restraint upon freedom of expression is considerable.

To combat actual suppression, defenders of the Bill of Rights may have recourse to the courts or, when legal action is not feasible, to counterpressure. In 1950 an Italian film, *The Miracle*, was duly licensed and exhibited in New York. The film, which won the New York film critics award for the best foreign picture of the year, told the story of a mentally disturbed peasant who believed that the father of her illegitimate child was St. Joseph. The exhibition of the picture aroused a storm of protest from Catholic organizations. Cardinal Spellman denounced it as blasphemous, the theater was picketed, and the Commissioner of Licenses, exceeding his authority, threatened to revoke the theater's license. The State Board of Regents, yielding to Catholic pressure, revoked the license previously granted to the film upon the ground that it violated a state statute against the depiction of "sacrilege." The lower courts affirmed the ban but it was reversed by the United States Supreme Court in a unanimous decision which declared the New York statute unconstitutional.

A different situation was presented by the controversy over the exhibition of the film version of Dickens' *Oliver Twist*. In

1948 Albert Deutsch, an American newspaper columnist, saw the film in England and wrote a column alleging that the portrayal of Fagin would fan the flames of anti-Semitism. Relying solely upon Deutsch's column (for no print of the film was available in the United States), the New York Board of Rabbis took steps to prevent the licensing and exhibition of the picture. In this effort, it had the support of other Jewish organizations. In opposition, civil libertarians, while upholding the right to denounce, to picket, and to boycott, insisted that suppression of the film amounted to censorship. The battle went on for nearly three years. The Motion Picture Production Code Administration, yielding to pressure, refused to give the picture its seal of approval. This denial of a seal was overruled by the Board of the Motion Picture Association and the picture was eventually released for exhibition though only after 800 or 900 feet had been cut.

It is interesting to note that the proceedings in *The Miracle* case caused Albert Deutsch, instigator of the agitation against *Oliver Twist*, to reverse his position completely. In a statement whose publication he authorized, he said:

> My own reaction to the successful effort to impose a ban on the film *The Miracle* revealed to me a contradiction in my own thinking about censorship. I could not honestly condemn a move to ban *The Miracle* and at the same time endorse a move to ban *Oliver Twist*. Free speech in any form involves inherent dangers, but the way to meet those dangers effectively is to strengthen our democracy—including the right of free expression—not to weaken it at any point.

Or, as Voltaire put it: "I disapprove of what you say, but I will defend with my very life your right to say it." It is in support of this position that the free speech advocate firmly opposes censorship in every guise, for he believes with Justice Holmes that "if there is any principle of the Constitution that more imperatively calls for attachment than any other, it is the principle of free thought—not free thought for those who agree with us, but freedom for the thought we hate."

## EDITOR'S NOTE

Mr. Rice completed this chapter in March, 1967. Subsequently, he agreed that comments should be added to point up certain new trends in mass communication which relate both to censorship and an expansion of the transmission of opinion and information to the public. Unfortunately, before these areas could be further developed, Mr. Rice died. The following observations are presented not as an expression of Mr. Rice's views, but as a stimulus to the reader's thinking about some of the new opportunities—and the dangers they may pose—arising in the mass communications field.

In the section on radio and television it should be noted that the rapid advances of technology have opened vast potentials for possible large-scale increases in the diversity of facts, ideas, and analyses made available to the general public. The experiments have left the laboratory and as intercontinental satellite transmission has shown, space can be utilized to beam programs from one part of earth to another. As the use of space for communication via satellite becomes more refined, we can expect it to serve not only as a relay for distribution of programs but as the source for direct-to-home broadcasts which can utilize hundreds of new channels in the spectrum. Positioned over different parts of the nation, theoretically, they could bring to local communities the mechanism for multitypes of programming; by breaking away from the technical limits imposed by the present spectrum's interference between ground stations, and by perhaps creating new networks of new stations, the full meaning of the First Amendment's support for free expression can be better realized.

Still another opportunity for increasing diversity through technological progress is illustrated by the rapid growth of

Community Antenna Television systems. First designed to use wire cables to beam on-the-air television into farm and mountain communities blacked out by obstacles of terrain and remoteness, the cable systems have quickly moved into large urban areas. Close to 2,000 local systems are now serving over three million homes, and pending applications for franchises nearly blanket the rest of the country.

Freed from the spectrum restrictions of on-the-air transmission, cable systems can present twelve or more channels to the viewer. Many systems are originating their own programs and producing full-time news, weather, and even business services. Looking to the future, perhaps within the next fifteen years, the same cables that carry television will also carry facsimile or printed newspapers as well as computer services, banking, and shopping. By integrating these cables into the equivalent of present telephone exchanges, the proliferation of programs and services would be limited only by the public's willingness to pay—whether directly, or indirectly, through taxes, subsidies, and advertising.

The growing concern over the quality of television fare, beyond the offering of regular and instructional education, has sparked the creation of the Corporation for Public Broadcasting, which, in part, reflects the view that government support offers new possibilities for new kinds of radio-TV programming. Already institutionalized by congressional statute, the CPB presents an opportunity for increasing the flow of information and ideas to citizens, although whether it can achieve this goal remains doubtful until the nagging question of funding the new corporation is solved. But since the financial scope of the challenge is so great, it is anticipated that the line will eventually run back to the public treasury, whose purse strings are controlled by Congress. This, in turn, raises the old bugaboo of political control. Since Congress is hardly the forum in which new, creative, controversial programming is encouraged—indeed it is the site of unbridled attacks on such programming—there are stumbling blocks on the road to the achievement of real diversity through the CPB.

However, the traditional civil liberties concerns about governmental control and the difficulties of financing do not dim the light that the space age has turned on. Fresh opportunities are opening up. The real challenge is whether or not citizens and their organizations have the ingenuity to find the means of solving these problems and the courage to insist that the airwaves, which, under the Federal Communications Act, belong to the public, be utilized in ways that will meet the public's need and interest.

In the section on newspapers, attention should be drawn to the discussion within academic and civil liberties circles as to whether or not the traditional fear and abhorrence of government sanctions on the print media, primarily on newspapers, should be altered. Minority political candidates have always complained of the lack of coverage of meetings or the chucking of press releases into the nearest editor's wastebasket. To this has been added the charges that unpopular, dissident groups (peace, civil rights) cannot purchase advertising space to present their controversial opinions, even when they have funds to use this technique. Appeals have been made to the press to recognize that while the First Amendment protects the editor's right to select news and advertising content as he chooses, he also owes the citizens a responsibility to further the fullest debate which the First Amendment seeks to assure. Too often such appeals fall on deaf ears. But is it too far-fetched to suggest that the public's need for a full political dialogue is so great that newspapers cannot reject out of hand paid advertisements from groups or individuals with whom they disagree or whom they feel are outside the community's pale?

This example is only symbolic of the general problem of the media making available more than already accepted ideas and opinions, including approved dissenting views. What can be done? The First Amendment says that Congress shall pass no law abridging freedom of the press, not that Congress may not act to promote more press accessibility to the people. Assuming that proper safeguards can be established to avoid the justified fear of government censorship, shouldn't we think, in affirmative terms, about how government might aid in assuring that the press' great power is used to increase public knowledge and thinking about issues that so vitally affect citizens?

We are living in an era in which government's responsibility to make meaningful the rights of citizens, in eliminating racial discrimination and substandard economic conditions, is now assumed. The First Amendment area is obviously more sensitive because of the danger of government manipulation of the press through its power to impose sanctions. But is this reason to reject automatically the frontier question of whether the affirmative obligation of government to help citizens enjoy the rights they are guaranteed can be appplied to the print and electronic media? Given the tremendous influence the mass media exercise in our political life and the trend toward common ownership of newspapers as well as TV, radio, and even CATV in the same community, the question of what can be done to have them better serve the needs of citizens is worth serious discussion.

—A.R.

# POLICE POWER AND
# CITIZENS' RIGHTS

by EDWARD J. ENNIS and
OSMOND K. FRAENKEL

Police activity, concerned with the prevention, detection, and prosecution of crime, is a fundamental activity of any government responsible for maintenance of law and order. In our society of diverse economic, social, and racial classes governed by written constitutions, exercise of this police power presents acute problems. The Bill of Rights of the United States Constitution embodies restrictions on the federal government in respect to such matters as the right to a fair trial; to freedom from improper arrest; the right to counsel; the privilege against self-incrimination; freedom from unreasonable searches; and the right to bail. These federal protections are repeated in various forms in state constitutions. To an increasing extent they are made directly binding upon state officials in decisions of the Supreme Court of the United States applying the provision of the Fourteenth Amendment of the United States Constitution that says, "nor shall any State deprive any person of life, liberty, or property without due process of law; nor deny to any person within its jurisdiction the equal protection of the laws."

Inevitably there are clashes between those who advocate zealous exercise of the police power to detect and punish crime and those who are concerned with the constitutional liberties of potential witnesses and suspects, whether guilty or innocent; these differences are resolved by the courts and, finally, by the Supreme Court of the United States. This case-by-case examination of the issues is the most important, but not the sole, means in determining the constitutional boundaries of police power and of individual civil liberties. Relatively few criminal cases reach the Supreme Court and its decisions are limited to the precise issues presented in particular cases. Even assuming that lower federal and state courts eventually apply these Supreme Court rulings, only a small percentage of criminal cases deal directly with abuses of police power. In most instances the defendant lacks either the will or the financial means to resist violations of his civil liberties. He usually accepts his fate or bargains for the most favorable solution he can obtain from the police, the prosecuting authorities, and the trial courts; he avoids risking the greater sentence which may be the price for asserting fully his constitutional rights by appealing to the higher courts.

Obviously it is necessary that the differences between exercise of lawful police power and the unassailable area of civil liberties be resolved not only by the enforcement of Supreme Court decisions but also by legislation and executive regulation of police and prosecution in respect to powers of arrest, search, detention and questioning of suspects, and the conduct of criminal trials. Let us first consider what the United States Supreme Court has done to extend the application of due process of law to federal and state prosecutions; then let us see what has been done and what should be done by legislation and executive regulation of the activities of police and prosecutors.

Both the Fifth and Fourteenth Amendments contain identical language forbidding the deprivation "of life, liberty, or property, without due process of law." As applied to criminal prosecutions these guarantees were primarily designed to insure fair procedures, that is, notice to the accused person of the charges and an opportunity for him to defend himself before an impartial tribunal. But in recent years the Supreme Court has greatly expanded the concept of due process. When dealing with federal convictions, the Court has felt free to go beyond strict constitutional requirements and, in its role as supervisor of the lower federal courts, it accordingly has set up rules of conduct which, however, are not applicable to state convictions since in reviewing these the Court is restricted to the constitutional safeguards. But in a series of decisions ranging over nearly half a century, it has included within the ambit of "due process" most of the specific guarantees dealing with criminal cases which are embodied in the Bill of Rights. For simplicity's sake we shall first deal with the restrictions peculiar to federal cases.

Perhaps the oldest of these was the 1914 decision in the Weeks case (232 U.S. 383) prohibiting the use in federal courts of material seized in violation of the Fourth Amendment. For nearly half a century it was not clear whether or not this prohibition was required by the Constitution and suggestions were made in some cases that Congress might change the rule. That uncertainty has, however, been laid to rest by the Mapp case, decided in 1961 (367 U.S. 643). And, as we shall see, the consequence now is that state courts as well as federal courts are prohibited from using illegally seized evidence.

Another rule that has, however, remained restricted to federal cases is the so-called McNabb-Mallory rule, first laid down in 1943 (318 U.S. 332) and elaborated in 1957 (354 U.S. 449), which bars the use in federal courts of statements obtained from an arrested person not promptly taken before a magistrate.

The Jencks rule (353 U.S. 657, 1957), which maintained that the defense was entitled to see statements made by a witness, originally was a judge-made one. But it was soon crystallized by Act of Congress (18 U.S.C. 3500). It also applies only to federal prosecutions.

In dealing with state convictions the Court has had to interpret the due process clause of the Fourteenth Amendment. Although that was adopted in 1868 it was not until the second decade of this century that this provision resulted in upsetting a state criminal prosecution.

In 1887 the Supreme Court rejected the contention of one of the defendants convicted of murder for throwing a bomb in the Chicago Haymarket riot that the jury had been unfairly chosen (123 U.S. 131). In 1915 it overruled Leo Frank's claim (237 U.S. 309) that he had been railroaded in a mob dominated trial. But in 1923 the Court (261 U.S. 86) accepted a contention that the trial of certain Arkansas Negroes for the murder of a white man had been a mockery because it was conducted under the influence of a threatening mob. Soon after that the number of state criminal cases considered by the Court began to increase and in the last few years such cases have become a very large part of the Court's business.

At first the Court was concerned with the fairness of the trial rather than with the conduct of prosecutors or police, but now it scrutinizes every aspect of the criminal process. Thus the earliest cases dealt with a conviction by a judge who had a financial interest in the fines he imposed (273 U.S. 510, 1927); with a conviction of Tom Mooney which, it was claimed, rested on the knowing use of perjured testimony (294 U.S. 103, 1935); with the failure to provide effective representation by counsel in the Scottsboro rape case (287 U.S. 45, 1932).

This question of counsel for indigent defendants resulted in a series of decisions that confused prosecuting attorneys and state judges with distinctions that were difficult, if not almost impossible, to reconcile. They stemmed from the 1942 ruling in *Betts* v. *Brady* (316 U.S. 455) which held that a state had to provide counsel in a noncapital case only if the circumstances—such as the youth or mental capacity of the defendant or the complicated nature of the offense—indicated that no fair trial could be had without counsel. So troubled were the state authorities with the uncertainties which that doctrine generated in the ensuing twenty years that when the question of overruling it was presented to the Court in the Gideon case in 1963 (372 U.S. 335), the attorneys general of twenty-two states asked the Court to lay down the simple rule that counsel should always be provided to indigent defendants. That rule has been applied retroactively and has resulted in new trials (or actual release) in many old cases in which a defendant was still in jail.

Indigent defendants are also entitled to free transcripts of their trial for purposes of appeal (351 U.S. 12, 1956) and that rule has also been applied retroactively (357 U.S. 214, 1958).

An important decision handed down in 1961 in *Mapp* v. *Ohio* (367 U.S. 643) changed the law of search and seizure by imposing on state courts the same restrictions that had previously been imposed only on federal courts, thus overruling a 1949 contrary decision (338 U.S. 25). But in 1965 the Court refused to give retroactive effect to the new rule, partially because the ban on the use of the evidence was primarily motivated to ensure police respect for the Constitution, and partially because the use of the evidence did not affect the fairness of the trial as, for instance, the absence of counsel well might (381 U.S. 618). The same principle was later applied to claims of infringement upon the privilege against self-incrimination (382 U.S. 406, 1966). And in 1966 (384 U.S. 719) the Court refused retroactive application of its far-reaching decision in *Miranda* v. *Arizona* with regard to the use of statements made by an accused person in the absence of counsel (384 U.S. 436).

That decision laid down rules for the guidance of the police: that a person in custody must be advised that he may remain silent and must be provided with a lawyer if unable to obtain one himself so that no statement made in the absence of the lawyer can be used unless it clearly appears that the person has waived having a lawyer. The following year the Court held that a lawyer must also be provided before the accused can be required to take part in a lineup (388 U.S. 218).

The subject of confessions had troubled the Court for many years. As early as 1936 the Court reversed a conviction that rested on a confession obtained by torture. As Chief Justice Hughes said (297 U.S. 278):

> The rack and torture chamber may not be substituted for the witness stand. The State may not permit an accused to be hurried to conviction under mob domination— where the whole proceeding is but a mask—without supplying corrective process. The State may not deny to the accused the aid of counsel. Nor may a State, through the action of its officers, contrive a conviction through the pretense of a trial which in truth is "but used as a means of depriving a defendant of liberty through a deliberate deception of court and jury by the presentation of testimony know to be perjured." And the trial equally is a mere pretense where the state authorities have contrived a conviction resting solely upon confessions obtained by violence.

An unusual case was that of Leyra (347 U.S. 556, 1954), who was convicted in New York of the murder of both his parents. While being questioned by the police before he was actually charged with the crime, he had complained of a sinus condition. The police captain told him he would send a doctor to help. In fact, the doctor was a psychiatrist who worked on Leyra for an hour and a half in a room wired to another until Leyra indicated he would talk. The captain, who had heard the conversation, immediately returned. Leyra then confessed to him and repeated the confession to the district attorney. New York's highest court reversed Leyra's first conviction, holding that the psychiatrist had practiced mental coercion so that the interview with him was improperly considered by the jury. That court ruled, however, that it was up to the jury at a second trial to determine whether the confessions to the captain and district attorney were similarly tainted. When the jury convicted, the state court refused to interfere. However, the United States Supreme Court decided that the later confessions were such an integral part of the psychiatrist's misconduct that they, also, could not be considered. Then, after a third conviction obtained without the use of any of the confessions, New York's highest court reversed on the ground that the only evidence against Leyra was suspicion (1 N.Y. 2d 199) —and he went free.

In 1964 the Court ruled in Esposito (378 U.S. 478) that it was improper to use a confession obtained while the prisoner's lawyer unsuccessfully tried to reach him. That decision rested primarily on the provision guaranteeing the right to counsel, while the later, broader Miranda case rested on the privilege against self-incrimination.

Another recent decision with respect to confessions has resulted in the reconsideration of many old cases. In most states the practice has been for the judge to tell the jury that it could not consider a confession if improperly obtained. This, the Supreme Court ruled in 1964 (378 U.S. 368), was improper because it was impossible to determine whether a verdict of guilty rested upon a finding that the confession was proper or upon other evidence outside a confession found to be improper. So now there must be a preliminary determination by the judge with regard to the confession.

Fundamental, of course, is the proposition that no one can be convicted for an offense not charged or when there is no proof of the offense that was charged. Thus, in 1937 Chief Justice Hughes, in the deJonge case (299 U.S. 353), declared that "conviction upon a charge not made would be sheer denial of due process." There, the Court reversed an Oregon conviction under its criminal syndicalism law prohibiting the advocacy of the overthrow of the government by force because there was no showing that the defendant, a conceded Communist, had advocated any illegal doctrine. He had merely assisted in the conduct of a lawful meeting held under the auspices of the Communist party.

The same principle has since been often applied—as it was to a charge of disorderly conduct based on the fact that the defendant had danced by himself in a restaurant without the manager or anyone else having objected or been disturbed (362 U.S. 199, 1960), and to the conviction of Negroes playing baseball in a park (373 U.S. 284, 1963). In the last few years it has been applied in a series of cases growing out of the civil rights protest movement. Convictions for disorderly conduct were reversed where defendants were peaceably "sitting in" (368 U.S. 157, 1961; 370 U.S. 154, 1962) or where unpopular views were expressed by people conducting a meeting and carrying signs in front of public buildings (372 U.S. 229, 1963; 376 U.S. 776, 1964). In other cases convictions for criminal trespass were set aside where Negroes refused to leave establishments at which they desired to be served (378 U.S. 146, 347—1964), or where they remained quietly in a library (383 U.S. 131, 1966). But convictions for refusing to leave jail grounds were upheld, by a 5 to 4 decision (385 U.S. 39, 1966).

One of the problems that is beginning to trouble the Supreme Court is the effect of mass media publicity on the fairness of a trial. In 1961 a conviction was set aside because the authorities stimulated the publicity (366 U.S. 717); in 1963 because of television showings of a defendant making damaging statements (373 U.S. 723); and in 1965 because the proceedings during the selection of the jury had been televised (381 U.S. 532). The subject again came before the Supreme Court in Dr. Samuel Sheppard's case from Ohio. There, a lower federal court ruled that there must be a new trial because of the impact of the publicity. The intermediate appellate court, however, held otherwise. But the Supreme Court reversed this court's decision (384 U.S. 333, 1966) and at his new trial, Dr. Sheppard was acquitted.

An instance of police conduct deemed so outrageous as to be a denial of due process occurred in the Rochin case (342

U.S. 165, 1952). There, the Court unanimously reversed a state conviction that had been obtained by using a stomach pump to recover drugs which the defendant had swallowed. But it upheld convictions, although blood had been taken, to determine whether the prisoners had been driving under the influence of liquor (352 U.S. 432, 1957; 384 U.S. 757, 1966).

There have been other situations also in which the Court has rejected a claim that a defendant had been denied due process—where a defendant had been kidnapped into the state (342 U.S. 519, 1952); and where police installed a microphone in an apartment (347 U.S. 128, 1954).

The Court refused to reverse the federal conviction of James Hoffa for jury tampering on his contention that the evidence had been obtained by planting an informer where he could listen to conferences between Hoffa and his lawyers (385 U.S. 293, 1967).

On the last day of the 1966 Term, the Court held that it was a denial of due process for New York to authorize electronic eavesdropping (388 U.S. 41, 1967). It has not yet passed on the validity of New York's law authorizing wiretapping on court order.

At the same term the Court relaxed the previously existing restrictions which banned the seizure of material that was only evidentiary in character (387 U.S. 294). The particular case in question dealt with the forceful taking of clothing and the Court expressed no opinion as to the application of the new rule to writings which might involve the privilege against self-incrimination.

In June, 1968, the Court upheld convictions based on evidence obtained when policemen stopped persons acting suspiciously where the circumstances justified the policemen's believing that there was a risk of danger to themselves or others. But at the same time it reversed a conviction where the police were looking for narcotics violators because the circumstances did not justify fear of violence.

The Court has dealt with the application of various specific guarantees of the Bill of Rights in ways not always easy to reconcile. Thus the requirement of prosecution by indictment does not bind the states, but as the result of very recent decisions, which we have already noted, the guarantees against unreasonable searches and seizures and the right to counsel do apply. Likewise, the Court has in the last few years concluded that the right to be confronted by witnesses (380 U.S. 400, 415—1965), the privilege against self-incrimination (378 U.S. 1, 1964), the right to a speedy trial (386 U.S. 213, 1967), and the right to a jury in serious offenses (391 U.S., 145, 1968) do bind the states. It is still uncertain as to whether the ban on double jeopardy affects state prosecutions (See 385 U.S. 76, 1966).

In the areas of self-incrimination and double jeopardy problems have arisen because the same acts may violate both state and federal law. For a long time the Supreme Court treated the states and the federal government as though they were foreign to each other and therefore ruled that a person questioned by state authority had no right to claim possible incrimination under federal law, and vice versa. Those decisions often created serious risks for persons compelled to testify under laws granting immunity. The resulting dilemma has now been largely eliminated by the realistic view that if Congress grants immunity it protects against state prosecution in the same area (350 U.S. 422, 1956; 364 U.S. 507, 1960). Since, of course, no state can grant immunity from federal prosecution the Court had to find a way to bring about a comparable result in cases of testimony compelled by state immunity laws: that such testimony cannot be used in a federal court (378 U.S. 52, 1965).

No similar solution has been found for the problem created by state and federal prosecution for what is essentially a single crime, as, for instance, possession of narcotics. But there are circumstances under which even the same sovereignty can conduct a second trial: where the conviction at the first is set aside at the defendant's instance (338 U.S. 552, 1950); or where the first trial proved abortive, because a juror was disqualified (155 U.S. 271, 1894); or where the judge stopped it because he believed that the prosecutor had overstepped the bounds of propriety (367 U.S. 364, 1961); or when the same holdup resulted in the robbing of several persons (356 U.S. 571, 1958). In the last two cases there were dissents by Chief Justice Warren and Justices Black, Douglas, and Brennan. In view of the subsequent change in the composition of the Court it is possible that the result might be different were similar cases again to arise.

The extent to which the privilege against self-incrimination prohibits prosecution for failure to register has produced some interesting variations in practice. The Supreme Court in 1953 (345 U.S. 22) held that the privilege did not protect a person charged with not having paid the tax required of gamblers and with not having filed a report since no disclosure of past gambling was required. But in 1968 the Court reversed itself (390 U.S. 39, 62, and 85). In 1965 the Court unanimously held that the Subversive Activities Control Act was unconstitutional insofar as it required individual members of the Communist party to register (382 U.S. 70).

In June, 1968, the Court ruled that no public employee could be dismissed because of a refusal to sign a waiver of immunity from prosecution, but the Court indicated that dismissal for refusal to answer questions relating to the employee's performance of his duties would be upheld.

There have been a number of recent decisions which may have important consequences: a conviction cannot stand if the state's highest court repudiates the theory on which the case was tried (382 U.S. 87, 1965; 384 U.S. 195, 1966); a convict who has been found insane while serving a prison sentence cannot be detained in a place for the criminally insane after the expiration of his sentence but must be given all the rights of persons committed civilly (383 U.S. 107, 1966).

In the far-reaching Gault case (387 U.S. 1, 1967) the Court ruled that juveniles were entitled to all the rights given to adults accused of crime.

Aside from Supreme Court decisions involving police power and civil liberties, progress has been made in the areas of legislation and executive implementation such as statutory provision for indigent defendants. But there is still stubborn resistance in other areas, including the regulation of procedure for obtaining confessions, on the ground that detection of crime will be seriously hampered.

Since 1937 the Judicial Conference of the United States (composed of federal judges assigned to consider reform of judicial procedures), the United States Department of Justice, and the American Bar Association have sponsored or endorsed proposed federal legislation for the appointment of paid counsel for indigent defendants in the federal criminal courts. The Sixth Amendment's requirement that the accused shall enjoy "the assistance of counsel for his defense" was imperfectly enforced in the past because, although the federal courts would appoint counsel for indigent defendants, there was no provision for paying them. State courts were not required by the Constitution to appoint counsel except in capital cases involving the death sentence. Reform proposals made no progress until, in 1963, the Supreme Court held that the requirement of the Sixth Amendment stipulating that the accused had to have counsel was now applicable to the state courts under the coverage of the due process clause of the Fourteenth Amendment. After this decision, Congress promptly adopted the Criminal Justice Act on August 20, 1964 (18 USC 20006 [a]), which provides for government-paid counsel for anyone charged with a federal violation or misdemeanor, other than a petty offense, who is financially unable to obtain counsel. In order to satisfy the constitutional requirements, New York (Code of Criminal Procedure, Section 308) and other states adopted statutory provisions requiring the courts to assign counsel to defendants financially unable to obtain counsel.

These statutory provisions, however, merely add to the constitutional right to counsel the practical requirement that the government must pay the lawyer for taking on a case of an accused indigent after he is charged with crime and not force the indigent to rely on the assistance of unpaid counsel appointed by the court. These provisions, however, do not deal in any way with the right of an accused, whether or not he can afford one, to have assistance of counsel prior to the formal charge of crime. Nor do they protect a person accused of a crime during the crucial period of police investigation of the alleged crime when the evidence is being procured in part by police questioning the suspect. There has been public debate between prosecuting authorities, including the police and some judges, professors of criminal law, and attorneys concerned with the protection of constitutional rights, on the question of whether a criminal suspect is, or should be, entitled to assistance of counsel in all cases before he is questioned by the police.

The police argue that a crime, when it is committed in secret without witnesses, can best be proven when the confession is "voluntarily" given by the "criminal" before he has a chance to receive legal aid advising him to invoke his constitutional right not to give a statement and possibly incriminate himself.

The policemen's assumption that a man will not confess to a crime if he is aware of his constitutional right to be silent is an inaccurate generality which ignores the many cases of persons who, knowing their rights, freely confess to the crimes they have committed. Indeed, it is difficult to assert that a confession is fully voluntary if the individual does not fully understand his right to remain silent.

In opposition to the police view that legal advice before questioning impedes criminal investigation is the civil libertarian attitude which maintains that suspects in police custody, particularly the indigent and those people who are ignorant or imperfectly aware of their constitutional rights, are pressured to confess to crimes they have not committed (or have committed) precisely because they are deprived of legal counsel that could point out to them their constitutional rights not to incriminate themselves. The civil libertarian view is that the only way to make this constitutional right against self-incrimination meaningful is to provide that no person, affluent or indigent, self-assured or insecure in dealing with the police, should be required to give any statement until he has consulted an attorney.

In the Miranda and similar recent cases mentioned above, the Supreme Court dealt with this problem by reversing convictions which had been based on confessions and admissions obtained after denial of counsel. At the same time, the Court ruled that counsel may be waived and did not hold, as it was urged to do, that no confession should be taken in the absence of counsel. The possibility of waiver of counsel, of course, now leaves open in particular cases a serious question of credibility when there is conflicting testimony. Police will claim, and defendants will deny, that there was a voluntary waiver of counsel and courts will be required to decide the issue on the unsatisfactory interested testimony.

These recent Supreme Court decisions, excluding confessions obtained in the absence of counsel unless counsel had been wavied, do not settle all the problems of pre-arraignment procedure. The American Law Institute, in a draft of a Model Code of Pre-Arraignment Procedure, has proposed to clarify and affirm the powers of the police to detain and question suspects who are without counsel. Opposition to this position had been stated, notably in June, 1965, in an exchange of correspondence between Chief Judge David Bazelon of the U.S. Court of Appeals for the District of Columbia Circuit and U.S. Attorney General Katzenbach. Judge Bazelon pointed out that the public interest in confession procedure is concerned with crimes of violence, such as robbery and assault, which are committed for the most part by individuals from the indigent and ignorant segment of the community and, in large cities and in the District of Columbia for example, largely by Negroes. He insisted cogently that a proposed provision allowing police questioning of detained suspects without counsel would legislate one law for the rich and another for the poor; it would allow those who could obtain counsel to do so before they were questioned, but would place no obligation on the government to secure counsel for indigent or ignorant suspects before they were questioned. Attorney General Katzenbach replied that the purpose of criminal investigation is to discover the criminals and not to produce equality of treatment or to advance a welfare program in legal services; he stated that police questioning primarily affects the poor because it is among the poor that such crime is found and that obligatory introduction of counsel at an early state of investigation would not aid separation of the guilty from the innocent but, rather, would aid the escape of the guilty.

Similarly, officials involved in the administration of criminal justice on the state level disagree on the importance of permitting the police to seek confessions from suspects without the intervention of counsel. Justice Schweitzer of the New York Supreme Court expressed the view, on the basis of his long experience in criminal cases, that confessions play a very small part in obtaining convictions. But New York County District Attorney Hogan, whose office prepares thousands of the criminal cases presented in that Court, disagrees; he states that restrictions on police who are seeking confessions hampers law enforcement. Chief Justice Weintraub of the New Jersey Supreme Court has commented that, in his experience, if police are compelled to make a lawyer available to a suspect before taking confessions, this requirement will, in effect, eliminate confessions because suspects will not confess after obtaining legal advice.

In examining these conflicting views, it should be noted that the objective of having legal counsel before confessions are sought is not to discourage all voluntary confessions but simply to eliminate either false or forced confessions. The objective is to assure that confessions, when obtained, will be truthful and voluntary after the suspect is informed of his constitutional right to remain silent. If we adhere to the view that only truly voluntary confessions are desired we cannot reject the procedure most likely to assure that voluntary character; namely, providing the suspect with legal advice before seeking the confession. The present alternative of "voluntary" waiver of counsel by the suspect involves inescapable doubts as to whether the suspect understands his rights to counsel and intelligently and voluntarily waives them. The only way to avoid this difficulty is to require counsel before the suspect is questioned. So long as the privilege against self-incrimination is maintained, it is difficult to argue that it should be circumvented by dubiously voluntary and dubiously knowledgeable waiver of legal advice of the right to remain silent.

Another aspect of the criminal process which requires further regulation to assure a fair trial for the defendant is the too frequent trial by newspaper, where the facts of the crime with which the defendant is charged tend to be exploited sensationally. The Supreme Court has recently pointed the way by reversing the state court convictions of Billy Sol Estes (381 U.S. 532) and Dr. Samuel Sheppard (384 U.S. 333) as denial of fair trial and due process of law because of the conduct of the prosecution and police in giving out prejudicial details about the defendants and the conduct of the trials which were subsequently publicized in the press. Nevertheless, regulations are needed to prevent such abuse of defendants in all cases, and we cannot wait for or depend on reversals by the Supreme Court of the United States in the occasional case on behalf of a wealthy or persistent defendant who can afford to appeal his case to the highest tribunal.

Professional canons of ethics, such as those which admonish attorneys not to resort to newspaper or other publicity concerning pending or anticipated litigation (Canon 20 of the American Bar Association), are dead letters honored in the breach; they do not govern police and other government employees, other than attorneys, who may be the source of publicity releases about a defendant.

Any efforts to prevent eager journalists from printing prejudicial information against a defendant tend to be discouraged on the basis that the constitutional freedom of the press is inviolate. The weapon of the English criminal courts, that of holding in contempt and severely fining newspapers which print such statements about a defendant as a confession of prior conviction until it is introduced into evidence, has proved most effective in restraining journalistic excesses, but this approach has been considered not to be available to courts in the United States to assure fair trials.

Various proposals have been advanced as a means of cutting off prejudicial material at its source in government investigative or prosecutive offices. The American Bar Association's Advisory Committee on Fair Trial and Free Press chaired by Massachusetts Supreme Judicial Court Justice Paul Reardon has recommended for discussion a revision of Canon 20. It would proscribe from the time of arrest, or from the time of filing a criminal complaint, the release by any prosecuting or defense attorney of any statement concerning (a) the prior criminal record; (b) any confession or admission by the accused; (c) identity or testimony of prospective witnesses and similar information; or (d) any statement about the trial except from the trial record. The Committee also recommends that this proscription be included in rules of all criminal courts, state and federal, and that violations be punishable as contempts of court. Such rules would extend to government personnel in addition to attorneys involved in the administration of criminal justice, and would add the sanctions of imprisonment or fine for contempt to the sanction of disbarment, suspension, or censure in disbarment proceedings. The Committee also suggested expanding the challenge to prospective jurors for cause to include not only those jurors who admit they have been influenced by adverse publicity about the accused but also such jurors who admit they have read such publicity, even if they deny it has affected them. The ABA has approved these recommendations.

In 1967 the Special Committee on Freedom of Press and Fair Trial of the Association of the Bar of the City of New York chaired by Federal Circuit Judge Harold Medina issued its final report, also recommending revision and expansion of Canon 20 to control publicity by attorneys; it suggested a voluntary code for police and law enforcement agencies and use of the judicial contempt power to control participants in actual trials. But in the interest of free press the Committee concluded that between arrest and trial the judicial power should not be exercised to control prejudicial publicity. Time will tell whether the more voluntary approach of the Medina committee or the more rigorous approach of the Reardon committee will prevail but it does appear that under the impetus of the Supreme Court Estes and Sheppard decisions some further controls on prejudicial publicity will be adopted in the interests of fair trial.

Still another aspect of control of police activities is covered by the proposals in many large cities across the country that charges of police brutality or other misconduct toward citizens should be reviewed by independent boards of civilians. At present, if a citizen wishes to charge a police officer with brutality or other misconduct his usual recourse is to try to bring criminal charges for assault or initiate civil actions for assault and battery. In several large cities, including New York, Chicago, and Los Angeles, citizens can make complaints to administrative boards established in the police departments and manned by high-ranking police officials. These remedies have proved to be incomplete and inadequate in satisfying the demands of complainants, particularly those of Negro and Puerto Rican minorities in our large cities, for fairer and more courteous treatment by police officers who for the most part are middle income members of the white majority, and who are socially and economically separated and estranged from the poor urban minorities.

Obviously, invocation of the criminal law, which is largely administered by the police, has proved to be an inadequate tool for controlling police misconduct. Substantial damages are paid every year in the wake of thousands of civil actions brought against police officers and the cities who employ them for false arrests and assaults. While statistics are not readily available, one study indicated that in 1963 over 300 civil suits were pending against New York City for police brutality and that over $100,000 was paid to a score of plaintiffs in such actions. Similarly, in Chicago there has been recovery of damages for police brutality. This judicial remedy, however, is insufficient in terms of the broad public for several reasons: it involves an expense which most plaintiffs are not able to afford; it involves the law's delay, which is psychologically and practically an incomplete answer to an outraged citizen's complaint of mistreatment involving manhandling or insults by a police officer; and it is not suited to cases not involving substantial damages for serious physical injury.

What is needed is a prompt administrative procedure to investigate and determine complaints. The accused officer should either be vindicated, or, if found guilty, made subject to disciplinary administrative procedure resulting in discharge, suspension, or loss of pay. The fundamental difficulty with administrative review boards in police departments today is that many complainants feel, reasonably enough, that police officials cannot be expected to conduct rigorous investigations or judge without bias complaints against subordinate policemen. In large cities, where there have been physical clashes between the police and minority groups engaged in protest demonstrations involving serious physical injuries, strong emotions pro and con have been aroused on the issue of independent review boards. Minorities are convinced that they do not get a fair deal from present police review boards. The police, supported by influential elements in the community, insist that exercise of their authority must not be reviewed administratively by civilians outside the police departments.

From the viewpoint of administrative law, it is a step backward to maintain that police officials, largely concerned with enforcement functions, can judge without any conscious or unconscious bias charges against their subordinates. In many other fields both statutory and practical standards have been developed to use effectively unbiased adjudication officers who are wholly separated from the enforcement responsibilities of their government agencies. It seems clear that civilian review boards outside the police departments are preferable to the present boards. In terms of civilized administrative law and from practical considerations, complainants must have faith in the fairness of the administrative procedure they invoke against government officers.

The principal objection voiced to independent review is that it dilutes a police commissioner's authority to discipline his subordinates and thus adversely affects efficiency in a paramilitary organization like the police. Such police organizations as the International Association of the Chiefs of Police and the New York City Police Benevolent Association adamantly oppose any independent review board. Actually, the procedure proposed is for the independent board merely to recommend to the police commissioner the action to be taken against a police officer. Final decision would be left in the commissioner's hands subject only to the influence that recommendations from eminent private civilians would have on the commissioner.

Independent boards were established in Philadelphia, Pennsylvania, by an order of Mayor Richardson Dilworth, and in Rochester, New York, by a municipal ordinance. The legality of both of these boards is under attack in the courts as constituting illegal interference with police authority. The attempt of Mayor Lindsay of New York City to accommodate the civilian and police interests with a board in which the majority (four members) were independent civilians and the minority were three police officials was decisively rejected in a city-wide referendum in the November, 1966, election by a vote of 1,307,738 to 768,492.

Police Commissioner Leary immediately re-established the Civilian Complaint Review Board made up of five officials of the Police Department who are not members of the uniformed force to continue the work of reviewing civilian complaints of unnecessary use of force or discourtesy. From July 1 to December 31, 1966, 541 complaints were received consisting of 277 complaints of unnecessary force (beating, pushing, kicking, hitting, and shooting) and the remainder dealing with abuse of authority and discourtesy. About one-half of the complainants were Negroes and Puerto Ricans.

In the wake of the 1967 summer riots in Newark, Detroit, and elsewhere, demands for civilian review boards of charges of police brutality persist and it may be predicted hopefully that gradually throughout the country the concept will be accepted that prompt and fair municipal machinery not wholly in the control of the police should exist to review complaints of police misconduct.

One way of achieving some independent scrutiny of alleged police misconduct could be the use of an ombudsman for that purpose. The use of such an independent public official to examine asserted oppressive governmental regulation was begun in Sweden over a century ago, continues to operate there successfully, and has also been inaugurated in England, New Zealand, the State of Hawaii, and Nassau County, New York. The ombudsman, a distinguished civilian with legal or governmental experience, may act on complaints or on his own initiative in the area of governmental regulation in which he has been granted statutory authority.

In large municipalities which have police department review boards but have rejected civilian or partially civilian review boards, at least some independent determination of the review system could be obtained if an ombudsman could examine the work of the police review boards, either on the complaint of a dissatisfied citizen or on his own initiative, and report his findings to the city authorities and the public. Such a practice would not interfere with the actual operations of the police, which is the objection usually advanced against civilian review boards, but would give those segments of the public which are not convinced of the impartiality of the police review boards an opportunity to obtain an impartial review of the work of the boards.

The uniformed policeman will continue to be the visible representative of government with which most people, particularly the poor and particularly people in trouble, will have most contact. To function successfully, police must have support from all segments of the community. Without it they cannot maintain public order unaided by military force. To obtain community support all segments of society must be made to understand that police are necessary guardians of public safety and not merely the paid agents of owners of protect property. Community relations between police and urban minorities must be improved by day to day demonstration that police will not violate individual rights in detection of crime and that when an individual policeman exercises his authority brutally or illegally rapid redress is available.

As police conduct improves and protects peaceful demonstrators in their right to assemble and express grievances, minorities will come more and more to realize that their grievances are not with the police but with stubborn social and economic conditions which deprive them of equal economic opportunities. The President's Commission on Law Enforcement correctly concludes in its report on "The Challenge of American Free Society" that far more must be done to meet the challenge of crime, including improved police training and practices, that our free society must act not only effectively but fairly, and that then "America can control crime if it will."

# VII

# A COLOR-BLIND
# COMMONWEALTH

by **LOREN MILLER**

In 1965, when a delegate to the White House Conference on Civil Rights tried to inject the question of the Vietnam conflict into the proceedings, he was repulsed by James Nabrit, president of Howard University, with the assertion, "I am not going to let you hang this albatross around the neck of the civil rights movement." The weight of Negro opinion is on Mr. Nabrit's side. The overwhelming majority of Negroes do not want civil rights questions confused with or even considered in the context of other issues, either foreign or domestic. The reason is implicit in the Nabrit statement; the other issue may repel prospective supporters of civil rights—that is, it may prove to be an albatross. This attitude presupposes that there are clear cut "civil rights" issues which are sharply and clearly defined and easily recognizable. It is easy to make out an opposing case and to demonstrate after a fashion that civil rights do not exist in a social vacuum but are intertwined

with, and are only aspects of, man's relationships with man in
our complex society. However, when Americans talk about
civil rights, they are talking about rights which are enjoyed by
others as a matter of course but which are denied, or impaired, for Negroes because of racial identity. There are a
wide variety of situations in which such denials or impair-
ments occur.

No white American has ever had to secure a judicial decree
in order to use or occupy his own home, live where he
chooses in an American city, ride in a Pullman car or in the
front end of a bus, attend a public school or a state-owned
college or graduate school, establish his right to have persons
of his own race sit on a grand jury which indicted him or sit
on the trial jury which heard his case, or eat in a public restaurant or a railway diner, cast his ballot in a party primary
election, vote in a general election without proving that his
grandfather was eligible to vote in a similar political contest,
use the facilities of a publicly supported hospital or library, or
swim in the ocean.

That is only a partial list of instances in which Negroes
have had to call on the courts—often the Supreme Court of
the United States—to vindicate rights or privileges enjoyed by
their white fellow citizens without question. In addition,
Negroes have had to scurry around to induce Congress, state
legislatures, and city councils to enact laws or ordinances, or
wheedle presidents, governors, and mayors into issuing executive orders or decrees enabling them to buy or rent housing in
the open market or to secure employment at their trades or
callings.

Of course, white Americans have had to carry their own
grievances respecting deprivations or impairment of constitutional rights and privileges to the courts, including the Supreme Court, but their complaints have been of a different
order than those voiced by Negroes. They have sought to preserve and extend such rights as freedom of speech and press,
trial by jury, exercise of religion, judicial fairness, safeguards
against unreasonable searches and seizures, scope of legisla-

tive inquiry, protection against self-incrimination, and kindred guarantees implicit in the Constitution or explicit in the Bill of Rights. White claimants have never had occasion to charge that their race or color had any bearing on the infringement of such rights, but their victories have redounded to the advantage of all persons, regardless of racial identification.

Negroes and whites alike have based their claims on constitutional grounds. We are a nation of Constitution worshippers who trace all of our rights to that document. Most of us agree that the Constitution is the "greatest document ever struck from the mind of man" and that properly interpreted, it safeguards the rights and privileges of every man without reference to his race or color. Moreover, we insist that every conceivable right or privilege is encompassed within its protection. Just as the fundamentalist seeks sanction for his every belief and action in the text of the King James version of the Bible, so we appeal to the Constitution to verify our every demand or justify our actions with respect to the rights and privileges we exercise or seek to exercise. But, like Holy Writ, the Constitution is silent on many specific issues. Where there are textual deficiencies, we find those rights or privileges implied in the vague contours of the due process of law clause, or in the equal protection of the law phrase, or, in the last eventuality, in the general welfare or privileges and immunities provisions of our fundamental law. We also agree that our Constitution makes ours a government of laws and not of men, and that all men stand equal before the law although everyday practices belie the latter precept in many ways.

Lawyers and laymen alike know that there is a difference in the quality of rights exercised by white persons in distinction to Negroes. They know that the Negro does not stand equal before the law with his white fellow citizen, a knowledge that leads most Negroes and many white persons to spend a great deal of time and energy in the quest for racial equality. Although both Negroes and whites agree that all rights and privileges are imbedded in the Constitution and its amendments, and although most of them agree in theory that such rights are identical for both groups, the practical differences that exist in the quality of the rights sought to be exercised are recognized in the language that is used to describe those rights where Negroes are concerned or where white persons are involved.

Rights which are freely exercised by white persons but are denied or impaired where Negroes are concerned are ordinarily referred to as "civil rights." Organizations such as the National Association for the Advancement of Colored People which strive to protect these rights are "civil rights organizations"; laws prohibiting discrimination because of race are "civil rights laws"; judicial decisions protecting citizens against segregation or discrimination are "civil rights decisions." In practice, the term "civil rights" means "Negro rights." Rights or privileges which are said to emanate from the Constitution or the Bill of Rights and in which race ordinarily plays no part are referred to as "civil liberties." Organizations designed to protect those rights, such as the American Civil Liberties Union, are regarded as "civil liberties" organizations and judicial decisions protecting or preserving them are "civil liberties decisions."

Popular distinctions between civil rights and civil liberties are more than exercises in semantics. They are a reflection of the generally accepted notion that all white persons are endowed, by the mere circumstance of having been born white, with a full complement of rights which can be neither circumscribed nor denied without affronting the Constitution, and that, on the contrary, Negroes have only such rights as the white majority chooses to dole out from time to time. The vulgar expression of that belief is expressed in the pollsters' question: "Do you think Negroes are going too fast or asking too much in their demands for civil rights"? The question is almost never rejected by the public as an enormous piece of effrontery even by persons who would deny that there is any difference in rights inhering in white persons as distinguished from Negroes. Those who think of themselves as the most liberal answer, "No, it is time '*we*' extended full civil rights";

the conservatives reply, "Yes, it is time 'we' called a halt"; while the middle-of-the-roaders have it that " 'We' must give 'them' every opportunity to earn 'their' rights." Each answer assumes that Negroes have only such rights as "we" extend from time to time. That notion is rooted in the historical fact that the original Constitution and as it was amended by the Bill of Rights did leave Negroes entirely at the mercy of white Americans.

The Constitution as written in 1787 recognized and protected slavery where it then existed. It contained no specific injunction against slavery in federal territories and Congress admitted new slave states fashioned out of territory ceded by the original states and carved out of the Louisiana Purchase. Neither the original Constitution nor the Bill of Rights afforded any protection to those slaves or their progeny.

There was no national citizenship except as a derivative of state citizenship—for example, a person was a citizen of New York and, as such, a citizen of the United States. But the Constitution contained no restrictions on the manner in which a state could treat its own citizens; each was free to impose racial disabilities at its own discretion. In the exercise of that discretion, most of the states, north and south, denied Negroes the right to vote, sit on juries, or attend public schools. Pennsylvania, for example, permitted street railways to bar Negroes; no state forbade discrimination in places of public accommodation. Slave states prohibited public assemblage by Negroes.

The Supreme Court decided in 1834 that the Bill of Rights, with its magnificent guarantees of individual rights, was a restriction on the federal government only and was not binding on the states. Finally, the Court decided in the 1857 Dred Scott case that Negroes, either free or slave, even those who were citizens of the states of their residence, were not and could not become national citizens. State control and jurisdiction over civil rights was declared to be absolute. Chief Justice Taney said there were two categories of citizens, state and national, with civil rights entirely under the control of the states without interference by the federal government. He summed up the case when he said that Negroes had no rights which a white man was bound to respect. The "unhappy black race," he added, "were separated from the whites by indelible marks."

The Dred Scott case pretty well mirrored public sentiment of its time as far as Negro inferiority was concerned and as far as the power of the states to curtail Negro rights at the whim and discretion of the white electorate was concerned. There was some opposition to its dictum that free-born Negroes who were citizens of the states of their residence were not and could not become national citizens. The abolitionists did dispute these views, but belief in Negro inferiority was overwhelming and, as votes taken after the Civil War showed, most white voters in northern states favored discrimination against the Negro in the matter of voting, attendance at public schools, service on juries, and other exercises of citizenship duties. What infuriated the North as far as the Dred Scott case was concerned was its holding that the Missouri Compromise was unconstitutional and that Congress lacked power to exclude slavery from federal territories. The North was determined to curb the spread of slavery.

It is often said rather glibly that the Civil War reversed the Dred Scott case. Well, not quite.

What the war did do was to settle the question of supremacy in favor of the national government if the federal government chose to exercise such power through proper constitutional amendments. Ours was not a confederacy; it was a union, an indestructible union, of the states. The federal government moved to exercise its newly established power through the Thirteenth Amendment abolishing slavery in 1865 amid anguished cries of Southerners that the amendment produced a "centralization of power and a consolidated Government . . . ." Lincoln's death, Andrew Johnson's intransigence, and the South's Black Codes reducing the Negro to semislavery thrust power into the willing hands of the abolitionists turned Republicans who controlled Congress.

Led by Thaddeus Stevens, John A. Bingham, and Charles Sumner, Congress went to work to reverse the Dred Scott case in its entirety. It enacted the Civil Rights Act of 1866, the first piece of legislation to make the term "civil rights" practically synonymous with the appellation "Negro rights"—a practice that has continued down to our own time. That Act ranged over the whole field and bestowed on Negroes the *same* rights—not equal rights or substantially equal rights, but the same rights—as were enjoyed by white citizens in almost every imaginable phase of citizenship.

In order to cement these newly bestowed rights into the Constitution and put them beyond repeal by some future Democratic Congress, the triumphant Republicans then wrote the Fourteenth Amendment, translating the Civil Rights Act of 1866 into constitutional shorthand. They secured the Amendment's ratification in 1868. In 1870 they wrote and forced the ratification of the Fifteenth Amendment, which opened the ballot box to Negroes. Each of the Civil War Amendments contained a telltale phrase providing that "Congress shall have power to enforce this article by appropriate legislation." It seemed to framers of the Amendments that they had wiped out what they considered the evil of the Dred Scott decision beyond possibility of legislative repeal or judicial interference.

Negroes were now free men and citizens of the United States *and* of the states wherein they resided. By its terms the Fourteenth Amendment protected all citizens against an abridgement of their privileges and immunities; it forbade denial of equal protection of law and of due process of law. Above all, Congress had put, or thought it had put, civil rights under the care and protection of the federal government. And Congress—not the Supreme Court, not the states but *Congress*—had "power to enforce" protection of those rights. It proceeded to exercise its newly established power by re-enacting the Civil Rights Act of 1866 and a spate of new legislation ramifying out into minute areas of the law. It climaxed its work with the Civil Rights Act of 1875, protecting the right to vote, forbidding discrimination in jury selection, fixing punishment for denial of constitutionally protected rights of Negroes, and proscribing racial discrimination by inns, theaters, trains, and all other places of public accommodation.

As originally proposed by Senator Charles Sumner, the 1875 bill also prohibited racial segregation in churches, schools, and cemeteries. The Senate struck out the church provision, apparently on the theory that it asked too much of Christians. The House deleted the provisions respecting schools and cemeteries. But most of the bill withstood attacks and crippling amendments. Senator Sumner could say in contemplation of its passage that thereafter "in all of our legislation" there would be "no such words as black or white . . . only . . . citizens." Apparently, the "indelible marks" found by Chief Justice Taney to separate "the unhappy black race . . . from the whites" had been erased. But Congress had reckoned without the judiciary.

The Supreme Court had been in eclipse since the Dred Scott decision, in the words of one of its most ardent admirers. There were many who blamed the Court for precipitating the Civil War, and its vacillating course during the war had brought heated charges that it was a "nest of traitors." As the moral fervor generated by a civil war that had turned into a war of emancipation ebbed away, the Court moved to reestablish its power. Cautiously at first and then with increasing vigor after the Republicans abdicated power and returned control of the South to the states in the 1876 compromise, the Court began substituting its judgment for that of Congress with respect to civil rights.

In a surprising series of decisions between 1873 and 1900, the Supreme Court restored the Dred Scott doctrine that there were two categories of citizenship—state and federal—with federal citizenship rights severely limited; held that civil rights remained under the jurisdiction of the states where they had always been; decided that the Fourteenth Amendment gave Congress no authority to interdict racial discrimination by individuals. The Court also restricted the Fifteenth Amendment to mean that the states retained control of the franchise and the ballot box with the sole exception that they could not impose racial tests for voting; cramped congressional control of voting legislation; held that the states could classify persons on the basis of race; and finally sustained the separate but equal rule which validated Jim Crow laws.

In defiance of congressional intent and purpose the Supreme Court had assimilated the color-caste system to the amended Constitution. Its action, as the first Justice John Marshall Harlan argued in a great dissent in 1883, made Negroes a "class of human beings in practical subjection to another class, with power in the latter to dole out to the former just such privileges as they may choose to grant." He foresaw that if the duty to protect the civil rights of Negroes was wrenched from the federal government and returned to the states, "we shall enter upon an era of constitutional law, when the rights of freedom and American citizenship" would not be adequately protected. He reiterated that warning in 1896 with the acid comment that "we have yet in some of the states a dominant race—a superior class of citizens, which assumes to regulate the enjoyment of civil rights, common to all citizens, on the basis of race." His warnings went unheeded.

The Supreme Court's holding that the Fourteenth Amendment did not authorize Congress to interdict individual discrimination undermined the whole structure of congressional legislation that had been enacted to protect the Negro in his exercise of civil rights. It meant, in effect, that the states had only to stand aside and do nothing while individuals or combinations of individuals banded together in voluntary or corporate form and practiced wholesale discrimination that reduced the Negro to helplessness and ultimately to poverty or worse. The Negro could claim the protection of the Fourteenth Amendment only when he could prove that the state participated in or lent its assistance to discriminatory conduct. As long as there was no state action, the Negro was helpless unless he could induce the state of which he was a resident to protect him and, of course, he could not do that in the Southern states where he most needed protection. Under the separate but equal doctrine, he had to make do with whatever facilities were offered to him unless he had the time, money, and patience to carry his case to the nation's highest tribunal; and at that level he would learn that equality of facilities did not mean identity of facilities. "Separate but equal" meant "substantial equality" and "substantial equality" was satisfied if the Negro's child was furnished a one-room, ungraded school while the white neighbor's child attended a ten-room, graded school, and that a wooden chair car with no facilities was substantially equal to a Pullman car with running water. State control of the franchise meant wholesale exclusion of Negroes from the voting booths: Louisiana's Negro voting strength declined 99 per cent after the Supreme Court validated evasive legislation that was deliberately and confessedly designed to disfranchise Negroes.

Negroes reaped the bitter harvest of the Supreme Court's nineteenth century rulings in the first three decades of the twentieth century. Segregation grew ever more intense. The Supreme Court approved the white primary as imposed by Democratic party rules and regulations; it indirectly approved state laws forbidding voluntary interracial association in schools, churches, taxicabs, and places of public accommodation. It stood aside and permitted judicial enforcement of racial restrictive covenants; it put its blessing on separate schools, and in the main encouraged the segregation system in almost every aspect of national life. Congress accepted the Supreme Court judgment that control over civil rights lay in the domain of the states and enacted no civil rights legislation between 1875 and 1957. The executive branch of government also gave in to Jim Crow and approved restriction of Negroes to the messmen's branch of the Navy, their exclusion from the Marine Corps, the Coast Guard, and the Air Corps, and strict segregation in service branches in the Army. Racial segregation became the rule in facilities maintained by federal departments in Washington.

Voluntary organizations took their cue from court decisions approving governmental classification by race and consequent permission to exclude Negroes from use of public facilities. Labor unions, trade groups, business organizations, professional associations, fraternal societies, PTA's, Boy Scouts, Girl Scouts, YMCA's, YWCA's, and a whole host of others excluded Negroes from their ranks. Unlike governmental units, voluntary organizations were not required to furnish "equal" facilities where they drew a color line. The Negro responded as best he could by forming duplicate, separate organizations. Meanwhile, Negroes had been driven from government, local, state, and national; they had no voice in decision making. Everything conspired to impress upon them the awareness that control of municipalities, the states, and the national government lay in the hands of white persons, just as it had prior to the Civil War. The Negro's sole legitimate concern, it seemed, was with accommodating himself to white aggression. If he deemed it onerous, he could only petition for, rather than demand, change. Under the American constitutional system, the only branch of government that had to answer his petition was the judiciary. The legislators and executive branch could simply ignore him. The Supreme Court—which had made the Negro its ward in that long series of decisions in which it had interpreted, and restricted, the meaning of the Civil War Amendments—was his only hope.

American whites of all shades of political opinion, with a few notable exceptions, agreed with the Negro that he had been deprived of participation in government and, most of them believed, rightly so. Even the Southern Populist movement, which initially protested the divide-and-rule tactics of the old planter class, slid back into a morass of racism and openly championed disfranchisement and degradation of the Negro. In 1908 William Jennings Bryan, the Great Commoner, told an approving Cooper Union audience that "The white man in the South has disfranchised the Negro in self-protection, and there is not a white man in the North who would not have done the same thing under the circumstances. The white men of the South are determined that the Negro will and shall be disfranchised . . . ."

The leaders of the Woodrow Wilson liberals—Carter Glass, Josephus Daniels, Oscar Underwood, and John Sharpe Williams—were bitter-end segregationists. Wilson himself clung to a belief in the Negro's inferiority. Sons and grandsons of abolitionists fell silent or admitted that their forefathers were in error in demanding full civil rights for Negroes. For the most part, conservative and liberal Americans alike dropped their demand for equalitarian statutes, consoled by a belief in William Graham Sumner's dictum that law ways could not change folkways. Historians, anthropologists, poets, novelists, social scientists, and psychologists poured out a constant, seemingly never-ending, stream of apologetics to prove that the Negro was inferior. The nation was caught in a paroxysm of racism that would have no counterpart until the rise of Adolf Hitler in Germany and apartheid in South Africa. The only dissent came from that minuscule minority of Americans that ultimately helped found the NAACP.

Of course, Supreme Court justices were affected by the social milieu in which they decided the law and fashioned their opinions. Conservatives and liberals alike accommodated themselves to racial segregation. Few justices of the Court have a shabbier record on civil rights than Oliver Wendell Holmes. Neither Louis Brandeis nor Benjamin Cardozo showed any understanding of, or genuine concern with, civil rights. Both ultimately acquiesced in segregationist judgments. Liberals such as Justices Charles Evans Hughes, Owen Roberts, Harlan Stone, William R. Day, and William Moody, to name the most outstanding, vacillated on civil rights. Their reputations as justices concerned with human rights rest on what they did and said on such civil liberties issues as freedom of speech and press, and with their attitudes as to the rights of states to experiment with social legislation under the Fourteenth Amendment.

Only one justice, John Marshall Harlan, persisted in the be-

lief that the amended Constitution forbade every semblance
of segregation, be it racial or anything else. He entered lonely
dissents in the 1883 civil rights cases, in *Plessy* v. *Ferguson*
when the separate but equal doctrine was enforced, in the
Berea College case in which the Supreme Court approved
state interdiction of innocent interracial association, in the
early voting cases. He protested in every instance in which
the Court put its seal of approval on restriction of the rights
of Negroes. Justice Harlan died in 1911 and the Negro was
without a champion at Court until the 1930's. Justice Holmes
has been enshrined as the Supreme Court's Great Dissenter,
but the title rightfully belongs to John Marshall Harlan, whose
magnificent dissents have become the law of the land in the
Supreme Court's recent civil rights decisions.

It was not until the 1930's that the Supreme Court began to
reverse the restrictive course it had pursued since 1873 in the
area of civil rights. It is true that prior to that time it had
stricken down state statutes designed to reduce Negro labor-
ers to semipeonage; it had invalidated grandfather clauses in
state election laws under which Southern states had sought to
limit the franchise to those whose grandfathers were eligible
to vote before the Civil War; it had interdicted racial zoning
laws and overturned criminal convictions where trial had been
mob-dominated. On the other hand, the Court's restrictive
decisions interpreting the war amendments and Reconstruction statutes far outnumbered its decisions favorable to civil
rights and had a profound effect on the thinking and attitudes
of those who were concerned with constitutional rights. Americans are almost idolatrous in their attitude toward the Constitution and tend to regard as moral and desirable that which is
said to be constitutional.

Assured over and over again by the Supreme Court that the
Constitution as amended condoned racial segregation, even if
it did not command it, the early proponents of civil liberties—as distinguished from civil rights—were little concerned
with racial issues. The American Civil Liberties Union did not
appear in the Supreme Court as *amicus* in the original racial

covenant cases of 1926, the Mississippi school segregation case in 1927, the white primary cases beginning in 1926 and lasting through 1935, the original professional school cases in 1938, the confession cases of the 1930's, or the original transportation cases. On their part, Negroes have displayed little interest or concern in Supreme Court cases involving traditional civil liberties issues. The NAACP has never defended or joined in the defense of Negro Communists or alleged Negro Communists caught in the net of the Smith Act or haled before legislative committees investigating un-American activities.

Beginning in the late 1930's and with increasing regularity in the 1940's and continuing down to the present day, the ACLU has proffered its assistance, often in the form of *amicus* briefs in all important civil rights cases. In many instances in the past few years, it has appeared for Negro litigants from the inception of litigation in what are commonly regarded as civil rights cases, that is, cases in which denial or assertion of a right hinges directly on the race of the litigant—cases which formerly would have been filed with NAACP aid and under its direction.

Recently, the NAACP has had to concern itself with so-called civil liberties issues in a few significant instances.

When Alabama and Virginia sought to hamper the fight against segregation through direct attacks on the NAACP, it defended itself by asserting those rights of freedom of speech and assembly which had been found effective in ACLU cases. It found those same decisions appropriate to fend off attacks by Louisiana and Arkansas. When Florida used investigation by legislative committees in its anti-NAACP maneuvers, the Association defended itself by adapting the law as developed by the ACLU in numerous challenges to congressional and state un-American investigations. Defense in the demonstration, sit-in, and related cases by the NAACP also drew into controversy rights of freedom of speech, assembly, and kindred civil liberties issues. But whatever rights it defended or sought to secure were described by the NAACP and mass media as "civil rights" simply because Negroes were asserting them.

The meaning of the term "civil rights" was further broadened as the Negro revolution of the early 1960's turned to new tactics and new problems. It has come to mean the right or privilege, or, perhaps more properly, the desirability of the Negro to be free from racial discrimination by labor unions in their apprentice programs, recruitment policies, and, indeed, in their internal promotional practices. Discrimination in the armed forces is branded a denial of civil rights. An employer who fails or refuses to hire Negroes is said to have invaded the Negro's civil rights. A real estate broker or a housing developer who refuses to sell or rent housing to Negroes is accused of hostility to civil rights. The short of it is that under today's popular usages, any discrimination against a Negro by a private person or by a political subdivision is spoken of as a denial of civil rights. What has happened is that the Negro's entire relationship with other persons in American society is increasingly conceived of and described in terms of civil rights. The Negro's persistent demand for "full civil rights" is understood by white and Negro alike to mean a drive for complete elimination of all customs, laws, practices, and traditions in every aspect of the Negro's life which set him apart or even demean him because of his color. This all-pervasive definition of civil rights and the term's application to every facet of the Negro-white relationships is eloquent testimony to the massive alienation of Negroes in our society.

In the effort to secure what are described as his civil rights, the Negro puts primary emphasis on law. In part this dependence on law stems from the cherished belief that the Civil War Amendments, properly construed, bestow complete equality on him. At the root of this belief lies a subscription to the doctrine of the rights of man: "all men are created equal and are endowed by their Creator with certain unalienable rights," that among these are "Life, Liberty, and the Pursuit of Happiness." The Civil War Amendments, the Negro believes, made him a Free Man and as a Free Man he is entitled to every right exercised by any other American. Furthermore, he thinks of the Civil War Amendments as equalitarian commandments binding alike on federal and state governments by requiring them to forbid all discriminatory practices which detract from equality and to enact all necessary legislation to insure equality. Thus, fair employment, or fair housing laws, and other equalitarian enactments are seen as required responses to constitutional directives.

The Negro's insistence upon use of law as the most effective agent in racial reform is heightened by his experience of what happened between 1875, when Congress passed the last civil rights legislation of the Reconstruction era, and the 1930's. During that period, the Supreme Court issued its long series of restrictive opinions on the scope and reach of the Civil War Amendments and almost no executive action was taken to protect Negro rights. Racial discrimination and segregation grew and flourished during that period, strengthening the Negro's belief that reliance on changes in the hearts and minds of men and on voluntary action offers little hope of change in race relations.

Dependence on law in the United States means dependence on courts under the doctrine of judicial supremacy, which gives the judiciary the power to interpret or invalidate legislative enactments or executive decrees. This is especially true in the case of the Negro who was reduced to a status of a ward of the courts by the old 1857 Dred Scott decision, and whose status as such was re-enforced by the Supreme Court in decisions designed to curb congressional power under the Fourteenth and Fifteenth Amendments and to re-establish judicial supremacy so badly shaken by the Dred Scott decision and the Court's attitude during the Civil War and early post-war years. As a consequence, the Negro has had to secure Supreme Court decrees in order to do what white Americans may do as a matter of course. As has been pointed out, no white American has ever had to resort to the courts in order to exercise such run-of-mine and everyday privileges as sitting where he chose in the public section of a court room or being addressed as "Mister" or "Miss" by a public prosecutor in a public trial. Negroes established these "rights" only by appeals to the Supreme Court.

Enforced dependence on the courts inevitably led to orientation toward legal struggle by the National Association for the Advancement of Colored People. There has always been, and there still is, much more to the NAACP program than concern with legal issues. But the organization learned early that its larger objective of first-class citizenship for Negroes could not be attained without destruction of segregation laws and constitutional interpretations that resigned regulation of civil rights to the states. In the early 1930s, the NAACP devised a plan for the systematic challenge of restrictive judicial decisions, particularly those of the Supreme Court, and it has pursued that program relentlessly since then.

In the past thirty years, the Supreme Court, at the urging of the NAACP and in deciding cases supported by it, forbade state use of coerced confessions; overthrew the white primary rule; interdicted judicial enforcement of racial restrictive covenants and prohibited levy of damages on those who signed and later violated such covenants. The government liberalized old rules respecting discrimination in selection of grand and trial juries; restricted discrimination by labor unions, particularly railroad unions; ordered the end of exclusion of Negroes from state graduate and professional schools; decided that racial segregation in any state-supported educational institution offended the equal protection clause of the Fourteenth Amendment; invalidated the separate but equal rule. Additionally, it protected the NAACP from state-sponsored attacks and from ouster by Southern states, and blunted attempts to use trespass and breach of the peace statutes to curb demonstrations and sit-ins. These and similar judicial victories helped create a new climate of public opinion in which Congress acted for the first time since 1875 and enacted civil rights laws in 1957, 1960, 1964, and 1965.

This new legislation established a Civil Rights Commission, threw new federal safeguards around the right to vote, authorized federal intervention to hasten desegregation of schools, permitted withdrawal of federal aid to state institutions and facilities where discrimination was permitted, prohibited discrimination in employment, and forbade discrimination in places of public accommodation and amusement. The Supreme Court's civil rights decisions only *helped* create the climate of public opinion in which congressional action was taken and hastened. Part of the change was also due to the demonstrations, freedom rides, sit-ins, pray-ins, boycotts, and similar actions that accompanied the upsurge in the 1960's of what we call the Negro Revolution. But it is well to bear in mind that to a large extent these activities were made possible by successive assaults instigated by the NAACP on old repressive laws that would have constituted impregnable barriers had they not been invalidated by the Supreme Court. There was also a radical change in public opinion, a change favorable to civil rights.

The shift in the climate of public opinion stemmed from the winds of change that were blowing all around the world. Within a half century, two world wars had been fought under the slogan of saving democracy and no matter what the cynics said, those wars with their democratic slogans had made a mighty impression on the minds of men. Colonialism and imperialism had collapsed within that half century in Asia and in Africa. Anthropologists, sociologists, and scientists had riddled old beliefs in racial superiority. All the races of mankind were represented in the United Nations, that Parliament of Man at once so impotent and so all powerful, so prophetic of the future and so unable to cope with present-day problems.

The change in public attitudes brought the Negro the assistance of many individuals and organizations in his quest for equality, including the ACLU, but the belief in racial differences inculcated by two hundred and fifty years of slavery and an additional century of racial segregation cannot be vanquished overnight. Unlettered and unenlightened whites still talk in terms of racial superiority and inferiority; a goodly percentage of the lettered and the enlightened move to the suburbs when Negroes pour into the centers of our cities and

talk in terms of racial pluralism. The Negro remains unassimi-
lated and by popular definition unassimilative. We expect him
to remain a Negro, as is shown by our population experts who
predict that in twenty or fifty or one hundred years, an increasingly large percentage of the American population will be
*Negro*. Massive ghettos and massive resistance to Negro residence outside the ghetto by every segment of the nation bear
eloquent witness to the racial division in our society, and to its
strength and durability.

The physical separation of Negroes and whites and majority
insistence upon maintaining the separation are matched by
racial distinctions in other aspects of our national life. The
Negro mortality rate is higher than that of whites; the Negro
illiteracy rate is higher; the Negro unemployment rate is
higher; the Negro poverty ratio is higher; the Negro median
income is lower—in sum, the Negro is obviously the disadvantaged member of our society. He has to think and plan in
terms of *Negro* rights and privileges until he attains parity
with other Americans. He bundles all of these wanted rights
and privileges together and calls them "civil rights," which is
as good a shorthand term as any, even if it does do violence
to technical legal definitions.

The Negro's bid for the support of white Americans in what
he regards as the quest for his civil rights is based on the
shrewd judgment born of experience that subscription to
democratic principles requires support from those who understand that denial of rights to Negroes imperils rights of the
majority. Imposition of the poll tax as a device to curtail
Negro voting disfranchised many poor whites; in Lowndes
County, Alabama, maintenance of the white jury system
wound up with jury service restricted to a small, selected circle of whites. Examples could be multiplied. There is the
added circumstance that the exercise of a right established for
a Negro may redound to the advantage of white persons. The
right to counsel that was vindicated in the Scottsboro cases
involving capital punishment for eight Negroes eventuated
many years later in a broadening of the rule to include the

right to counsel in all state felony proceedings. The recent Supreme Court ruling severely restricting the use of confessions and admissions of defendants traces back to a ruling against coerced confessions in a case involving Mississippi Negroes. No constitutional ruling is an island entire unto itself.

Similarly, civil rights statutes that were pioneered to protect Negroes against discrimination in employment or in the sale or rental of housing protect other minority groups as well.

The concentration of Negroes in large cities in populous industrial states gives Negro voters a balance of power advantage in state and national elections. Despite that advantage, Negroes, in most instances, need the assistance of white Americans in their civil rights battles at the polls. That outside assistance has often proved invaluable in judicial contests. None but the most intransigent Black Nationalists want to terminate an alliance that has been so fruitful in the establishment of civil rights, although there are many Negroes, perhaps most of them at this particular time, who insist on Negro leadership in the strategy and tactics of the civil rights fight.

The forecast is for increasing cooperation between civil rights organizations such as the NAACP and civil liberties groups such as the ACLU in impending struggles for civil rights; but this does not mean that the distinctions between civil rights and civil liberties are going to be blurred over. As long as the term "civil rights" remains synonymous with the appellation "Negro rights" and as long as racial divisions persist in American life, the distinctions will remain, seeming to narrow in times of racial peace and to gap wider in times of racial strife such as our present period. There are other divisive factors. For example, Negroes led by the NAACP have opposed jury trials for violators of court decrees in civil rights cases out of their knowledge that Southern juries won't convict such violators, while the ACLU has supported such jury trials out of its principle position on that issue. The NAACP has demanded censorship of such movies as *Birth of a Nation* while the ACLU has held fast to its position against censorship. Those differences will persist.

Negro civil rights groups are going to be driven to demand preferential treatment in public and private hiring practices in order to narrow the gap between them and white persons. There is every prospect that the ACLU will oppose such treatment on the ground that it is mere discrimination in reverse. These differences do not presage bitter conflict, but they do forecast continuation and some widening of the disagreement between proponents of "civil rights" and supporters of "civil liberties." There will also be ruffled feelings and some quarrels as Negroes insist on pursuing their civil rights objectives to the ultimate end of complete equality, against the counsel of those who advise caution.

Increased strife and bitterness lie ahead as the struggle for civil rights moves toward a climax. It will demand more time and more energy from Negroes. As more time and more energy are exacted, the Negro will become increasingly unwilling to embrace issues that lie beyond the boundaries of the civil rights movement as it is defined at the time and he will be less inclined to take a stand that may turn out to be an albatross around the neck of the civil rights movement. Paradoxically enough, many issues now excluded from the Negro's concern will intrude on him as he pushes his way into the mainstream of American life. That dilemma will be resolved by the semantic device of describing these new issues as civil rights problems. The Student Non-Violent Coordinating Committee (SNCC), for example, reduced the Vietnam conflict to a civil rights issue by the simple device of saying that soldiers should not be sent to Asia when they were needed to protect Negroes in Mississippi! Its cry of Black Power is only a device to elect Negro office holders who, in their proper turn, will protect civil rights of Negroes. Once issues are defined in terms of civil rights, Negroes will tackle those questions through their civil rights organizations.

The sum of the whole matter is that the nation is quite a distance away from the ideal of a color-blind commonwealth. Constitutional rights are still denied or curtailed because of race or color. Most Americans still agree with Chief Justice Roger Taney's century-old dictum that "the unhappy black race are separate from the white by indelible marks" and cling tenaciously to the belief that it is within the competence of the majority to determine whether the Negro is "going too fast" or "demanding too much" in his assertion of rights and privileges supposedly guaranteed by the Constitution to all citizens. The Negro cannot acquiesce in that judgment that whites may bestow or withhold citizenship rights as they bestow charity on the less fortunate. To do so would be an admission on his part that his is a second-class citizenship; it would be an acceptance of the validity and desirability of the color-caste system and an admission that the caste system is assimilated to the Constitution as amended by the Thirteenth, Fourteenth, and Fifteenth Amendments. On the contrary, the Negro must continue to assert that his rights are identical—not equal to or substantially equal to—but identical and coextensive with those of white persons even if he cannot enforce that claim for that moment. He must insist that whites can no more render valid judgments that he is moving too fast or demanding too much in the way of constitutional rights and privileges than he could render a contrary judgment that such rights and privileges of white persons should be curtailed to suit his whims or prejudices. It appears to the Negro that since the rights he claims are coextensive with the rights of all citizens, he enlarges the rights of all Americans as he attains his own ever-expanding and consistently redefined "civil rights."

The Negro is convinced by historical evidence that unless he pursues his own objective of achieving first-class citizenship through an unrelenting quest for civil rights, other Americans will neglect the problem because of lack of understanding, or hostility, or indifference. He fears and resists involvement in other issues that may detract from his primary effort to attain his own goal whether the distraction is threatened by concern with Vietnam, or denial of freedom of speech, press, or religion, or rights of unpopular political parties or members of such parties. As he sees it, all white persons are members of a dominant and advantaged majority, able or potentially able to shift for themselves. The folk Negro looks askance at a white person who complains of deprival of his rights: "Been free, white, and twenty-one all his life, ain't he?" America, the Negro reasons, has made him a *Negro* and saddled him with peculiar problems growing out of his strait jacket status for more than three hundred and fifty years. Since he must remain a Negro in the foreseeable future, he believes he must ignore or at best soft pedal other issues and concentrate his attention on finding solutions to the problems that arise out of his status, that is, to what he calls civil rights problems. There will be time enough, he thinks, to tackle problems that confront all Americans, *as Americans,* when he is admitted to the status of an American.

# VIII

# BLUE-COLLAR
# DEMOCRACY

## by MICHAEL HARRINGTON

The American labor movement provides constitutional rule to
more citizens in this country than any other institution except
the federal government itself.

The unions have created, in Clark Kerr's phrase, a "two
party system governing the life of the workplace." In the
process, the autocratic and arbitrary right of management to
hire, fire, and regulate workers has been profoundly modified
and there has been an enormous gain in freedom—in social
and economic civil liberty, if you will—for the members of
these organizations. In addition, labor has a long tradition of
fighting for social legislation which effects the lives of many
who have never belonged to a union and never will. In areas
like aid to education, medical care, social security, and antipoverty measures, the political power of the organized workers has been a crucial element in achieving democratic
reforms.

Quite often analyses of the state of civil liberties within the unions ignore, or, in the case of economic conservatives, willfully conceal these basic and fundamental facts. That is why I want to emphasize it so strongly at the very outset of this chapter.

At the December, 1967, convention of the AFL-CIO, it was reported that 14.3 million Americans, or 18.6 per cent of the work force, belonged to the Federation affiliates. And this figure omits, of course, the considerable number of unionists outside the AFL-CIO, most notably the more than a million and a half who carry Teamster cards. Moreover, there are many signs that the trend toward a declining percentage of union members in the labor force is now being reversed. The Kennedy-Johnson boom in the sixties made significant inroads on the unemployment which was chronic in the fifties (though in this writer's opinion, a level of 4 per cent unemployment as the official rate is a disaster for the black and white poor and the many others who are just a little better off than they are). As a result, the huge industrial unions like auto and steel exceeded their membership figures of 1955–57. And, of perhaps even greater future significance, unions have been rapidly expanding in the fastest areas of job generation: education and health services, and government.

In other words, it is wrong to assume, as many have in recent years, that trade unionism in the United States is permanently on the decline, and it is even quite possible that there will be a marked labor revival in the coming period.[1] Since this is the case, the issue of civil liberties within the unions defines one of the most important dimensions of freedom in the society as a whole.

By saying that labor has made an enormous, and continuing, contribution to the liberty of Americans, I am not, as will be seen in a moment, arguing that there is no need for democratic reforms within the unions. That need most certainly exists and hopefully this chapter will suggest the broad lines

[1] See my *Toward a Democratic Left,* Macmillan, 1968, Chapter X, for a more extended discussion of trends and probabilities.

of a response to it. But I do believe that these changes can only be effectively achieved through the action of the trade unionists themselves and those clearly sympathetic to their cause. Too often in the recent past, as the next section will make clear, those who most loudly proclaimed their devotion to the civil liberties of the individual union members were the same people who had done the most to hinder, or even destroy, the unions. When the advocacy of due process and freedom thus becomes a screen for reactionary economics, there can be no real democratic gain.

Perhaps this point can be made more clearly by an oversimplified but relevant contrast to two approaches to the problem of civil liberties within the unions. In one view it is necessary to challenge the tyrannical power of labor bosses who lord it over helpless but hostile members. The experience of the past twenty years, from the passage of the Taft-Hartley Act to the present, has shown this to be a self-serving and false myth propagated by the opponents of labor. In another view, which is mine, it is precisely because of its character as a democratic force in the society that the unions must not only accept but seek democratic reforms. This goal can be furthered by government action which puts a premium on voluntary internal change—but only if the decisions are made in a context sympathetic to the social and economic aims of the unions.

Concern over the civil liberties of union members within their own organization is of fairly recent origin. In understanding why this is so, and in identifying the conservative bias which so often animated drives for democratic reform, one gets a feel for the political realities which influence labor attitudes on due process within the movement. Even more to the point, the historical data teach an object lesson on how *not* to proceed in seeking to enlarge rank-and-file freedom.

From the very beginnings of trade union organization until after World War II, the balance of economic and political power was weighted so much in favor of management that the issue of the worker's rights vis-à-vis his own leaders hardly ever arose. There were, to be sure, vigorous internal battles between the followers of Gompers, the Socialists, the revolutionary syndicalists of the IWW, the political Catholics, and many other factions. Yet the most basic fact of life was the relative weakness of the workers and the strength of management.

As a result of this situation, many of the early unions were secret societies and discipline was based on that of the underground rather than on the model of judicial process in the larger society. The success of labor organization, particularly in the thirties, gave the workers enough power to defeat the crudest forms of management violence—Pinkertons, labor spies, the national guard—but the heritage of thinking of the union as a "combat" unit with military rules rather than as an organization with peace-time democratic rules still persisted. As Arthur Goldberg put it in 1959 (when he was still associated with the AFL-CIO):

> In discussion of union democracy it is often assumed that the ideal would correspond to democracy as practiced in our political institutions . . . if there is an analogy to political government, the analogy is to a political government which may simultaneously face uncertainty as to its continued existence, that is, face a revolution, and which is periodically at war.[2]

More recently, Gus Tyler expanded on this point and gave it a sociological dimension in *The Labor Revolution*. The unions, Tyler argues, "tend to be monosocial (like a parish church); to be combative (like an army); to be administrative (like a governmental agency); and to be market oriented (like a business). Taken together, these traits form a strong natural bent in established unions toward the 'one party' system, resting in the hands of an administrative machinery."[3]

Tyler does not, as will be seen, use this analysis in order to

[2] Arthur J. Goldberg, "The Trade Union View," *Labor in a Free Society*, Michael Harrington and Paul Jacobs eds., University of California Press, 1959. p. 106.

[3] Gus Tyler, *The Labor Revolution*, Viking Press, N.Y., 1967, pp. 240–241.

excuse the lack of democracy in the unions and he is quite frank about the very limited perspectives for completely voluntary self-reform from within labor. But he and Goldberg define an important aspect of the American union attitude toward "outside" regulation. In part, these same tendencies can be found in all of the democratic labor movements of the world. But in part, the American unions exhibit them to a particularly marked degree. In countries where labor organized a political party at a fairly early date, the unions did not regard the state apparatus as *necessarily* hostile to their interests. So it is, for example, that the Australians have accepted an extraordinary—from an American point of view—measure of governmental intervention into union affairs. But in the United States, where the government typically played the role of strike breaker in the formative period of labor organization, the sociological factors making for homogeneity, combativeness, and bureaucracy were reinforced. It was, after all, only in the last generation that laws were ever used for the workers.

This historic enmity toward any laws which would regulate the internal life of unions, even in the name of freedom, was made even stronger when the most vocal champions of civil liberties for union members in the post-World War II period turned out to be equally militant advocates of curtailing union freedoms as a whole. This seemed to confirm the bitter labor conviction that sermons on due process were a pious way of proposing the destruction of unions.

Part of the problem was that the conservatives actually believed their own most extreme horror stories. It is clear in retrospect that the sponsors of the Taft-Hartley Act thought that the requirement of free secret elections under the NLRB before a union shop could be granted would result in a mass exodus of workers from their unions. And yet, of the 46,146 elections held between 1947 and 1951, 97 per cent decided in favor of the union shop.[4] Even Senator Taft himself came to

[4] *Labor Today,* by B. J. Widick, Houghton Mifflin Company, Boston, 1964, p. 72.

realize how wrong his assumptions had been. But by the time he understood the reality, the unions felt that they had one more proof that the call for "democratic reform" was inevitably a tool of management disruption.

This attitude was further corroborated by the history of right-to-work legislation, the very title of these laws being, of course, a deliberate attempt to mislead voters. They did not guarantee a right to work (in the campaign of 1944, Franklin Roosevelt had proposed a legal obligation for the society to provide a man with a job and the unions, of course, supported him enthusiastically). And once more, the most bitter foes of the labor movement attempted to present themselves as advocates of the liberty of the individual worker. In those states where union organization had deep roots, the workers overwhelmingly rejected their self-styled friends whenever they got the chance. In the elections of 1958, the presence of right-to-work propositions on the ballot in Ohio, California, and other industrialized areas generated such a large labor turnout that the elections of that year also returned the most liberal Congress since the New Deal.

The Landrum-Griffin Act (the Labor-Management Reporting and Disclosure Act of 1959) followed the familiar postwar pattern. The effective strategy committee for the law—and its bill-of-rights provisions was one of its most controversial sections—was composed of a coalition of Southern Democrats and Administration Republicans (this was, of course, a striking example of the famous "Dixiecrat-Republican" alliance which played such an important role on the Hill from 1938 to 1965 and once again from 1966 to the present). The high command was composed of House Rules Committee Chairman Howard Smith and House Labor Chairman Graham Barden for the South, and House Minority Leader Charles Halleck and President Eisenhower's assistant Edward McCabe for the Republicans.[5] Such sponsorship would hardly convince

[5] For a general account of the legislative history of Landrum-Griffin, see *Power and Politics in Labor Legislation*, by Alan K. McAdams, Columbia University Press, New York, 1964, *passim;* for the account of the strategy committee, *cf.* p. 176.

trade unionists that the talk about personal freedom was anything but the usual smoke screen for antilaborism.

In point of historical fact, the supporters of a bill of rights for union members were by no means confined to the political right and the foes of labor. The American Civil Liberties Union had long defended trade unionism as a most important democratic institution in the society and was in favor of carefully drawn up legislation to guarantee certain membership freedom within labor organizations.[6] And yet the almost monolithic opposition of the labor leadership to federally mandated reform was clearly predicated on the assumption that the real political motivation of the Landrum-Griffin majority was conservative rather than libertarian.

This brief survey of union attitudes toward legislation requiring civil liberties within labor organizations has obvious relevance for the sincere advocates of reform. As unions have become somewhat more secure and have taken on important administrative and economic functions in terms of establishing seniority, wage rates, working conditions, and the like, the old image of labor as a guerrilla movement must be used quite selectively. It still obviously applies to organizing efforts like those among the migrant farm workers. The growers have employed the most ancient tactics of union busting—including the discriminatory use of the state police power. But it does not hold true in some of the giant unions which, out of the practical necessities of collective bargaining, have developed bureaucratic structures.

And yet, it makes no sense simply to denounce the established labor leadership for their cultural lag when they view all congressional attempts at reform with hostility. For it is true that the major political leaders who sought to force the legitimate issue of the worker's freedom did so for the illegitimate, antidemocratic purpose of impeding, or destroying,

[6] See the compilation of Statements by the American Civil Liberties Union, March, 1963, for the relevant documents; also *cf.* McAdams, *op. cit. supra,* p. 84, for the role of Professor Monroe Freedman, a partisan of the ACLU position (and husband of a union staff economist) in the Landrum-Griffin dispute.

unionization. And the strategic corollary is that the initiative for protecting the member's personal rights can only come from those institutions—like the ACLU—and individuals which have an unambiguous record in defense of labor's collective rights.

Given this historical and tactical perspective, we can now turn to the actual state of freedom within the American unions, particularly in the period since the passage of the Landrum-Griffin Act.

On the whole, the Landrum-Griffin "Bill of Rights" [7] has not radically altered the internal life of the American labor movement. In part, this is the case because the framers of the law, like Senator Taft before them, had an image of enslaved workers tyrannized by union bosses which had little to do with reality. In part, the law has not been particularly effective because of its own ambiguities and also because of the extremely cautious way in which the Department of Labor has applied some of its provisions.

At the time the Landrum-Griffin Act was passed, there seemed to be little vitality within the labor movement. The presidents of the various affiliates of the AFL-CIO had either founded their unions or inherited them (in a political sense —though the passage of power from father to son was not unknown). The members of the Dixiecrat-Republican coalition who forced the law through then assumed that the main force for democracy would be the intervention of the federal power from the outside. In point of fact, the extraordinary amount of democratic change which has taken place since 1959 has been largely the result of the militancy of the membership in challenging their leaders.

So it is that in the very recent past, major incumbents, in-

[7] The "Bill of Rights of Members of Labor Organizations" is Title I of the law, and provides "Equal Rights" for participation in union affairs; "Freedom of Speech and Assembly" specifies exactly how dues increases shall be voted; asserts the right of the member to sue the union under certain circumstances; and establishes "Safeguards Against Improper Disciplinary Action." For the full text, *cf.* McAdams, *op. cit. supra,* p. 305 ff.

cluding international union presidents, have been defeated in the IUE; Steelworkers; Teachers; Machinists; State, County, and Municipal Employees; Paperworkers; Pulp-Sulphite. And there have been vigorous struggles within the painters, musicians, operating engineers, marine engineers, and maritime deck officers unions. With a few significant exceptions, which will be dealt with shortly, these insurgencies succeeded not because they were aided by the federal government but because they mobilized a new, democratic majority within the various unions effected.

"Labor union locals," *The Wall Street Journal* reported in June, 1967, "are rebelling against their national parent organizations as never before . . . . Militant younger members increasingly are pressing for local rejection of contract settlements endorsed by national officers." So it was that in 1966 the members of the International Association of Machinists turned down contracts recommended by their national leaders and endorsed by President Johnson (the implications of this action will be considered in greater detail shortly). And during the 1967 auto negotiations, dissidents within the Auto Workers Union publicly campaigned for rejection of the bargain which had been negotiated by union president Walter Reuther. Reuther took on the oppositionists in public debate and carried the vote with the membership.

Indeed, most observers agree that a rank-and-file feeling that union decisions were being taken without their participation was a major factor in the success of I. W. Abel's bid for the presidency of the United Steelworkers Union. The USW has modified its constitutional structure in order to give a greater voice to members at the local level.

Most of the unions involved in the democratic conflicts just cited are major affiliates of the AFL-CIO. If one would follow out the analogy between union and federal democracy, then the last five years or so in the labor movement have witnessed the equivalent of a change in statehouse rule within five of the ten largest states. And this is a testimony to a much greater internal union vitality than any of the framers of the

Landrum-Griffin Act might have imagined. Their myth of labor monolithicism has been as discredited as Senator Taft's convictions that workers, given a free choice, would desert their unions.

And yet there is still a considerable way to go if truly democratic freedoms are to be guaranteed to every union member. Consider some of the evidence.

In some of the cases of democratic change which were just noted the conflict was not so much between rank and file, or oppositionist outs, and leaders, as it was between wings of the leadership. This was, for instance, the case in both the IUE and the Steelworkers. In the case of the IUE, the dispute was settled, in part, as a result of a court ruling ordering a recount of the ballots. It is, of course, a democratic strength when a labor union provides a mechanism for resolving disagreements at the top. But that does not necessarily guarantee the rights of the individual members.

In other cases, an extraordinary dedication was required on the part of those who challenged the leadership. The battle which led to the election of Frank Schonfeld as head of Painters District Council No. 9 in New York City required a legal struggle against a union trusteeship—imposed when the incumbent was indicted by a grand jury for receiving bribes—and a court-supervised election. In the fight within the West Coast painters in San Francisco, the opposition leader, Dow Wilson, was murdered. James Morrissey, an opponent of the union administration in the National Maritime Union, was beaten by hoodlums two weeks before the union convention in 1966 and not too long after he had amassed a considerable number of votes in a bid to become Secretary-Treasurer.

As the American Civil Liberties Union commented at the time of the attack upon Morrissey, "The ACLU, of course, takes no position on the merits of the dispute within the National Maritime Union. Nor are we in a position to establish, by independent inquiry, the accuracy of Mr. Morrissey's contentions with respect to harassment, intimidation, and alleged frameup attempts. However, the brutal attack on him lends sufficient credence to his allegations to seek further information on this matter . . . ." There was no answer from the NMU.

Both Morrissey and another opponent of the leadership, Gaston Firmin-Guyon, were forced out of the union in 1967 (Morrissey was "dropped" from membership on a technicality; Firmin-Guyon was expelled after a trial which he alleges was a frameup). At the same time, the Department of Labor had initiated a suit to invalidate the NMU elections on the grounds that the political process within the organization was illegally restrictive.

On the West Coast, a struggle has been going on since 1963 between Harry Bridges, president of the Longshoreman's union, and San Francisco longshoremen who had been fired without due process and through a discriminatory procedure arranged jointly by management and the union.[8] Most of the men involved were Negroes and their exclusion from the benefits of the "automation agreement" between the union and management is a particularly severe blow for them. As of this writing, they had had to fight for four years and carry their case to the U.S. Court of Appeals for the Ninth Circuit —and they still have not been guaranteed their rights.

There are other examples which could be cited, yet the main point is plain enough: despite the remarkable democratic vitality within the labor movement in recent years, there are still a significant number of cases in which individual oppositionists, or opposition caucuses, must go to extraordinary lengths in order to defend their basic democratic rights. And, the rights which are theoretically guaranteed under Landrum-Griffin have not been vindicated in practice. (I am concerned here with the civil liberties of union *members* and have therefore excluded the very important issue of racial exclusion from membership. In thus concentrating on

[8] I must "declare an interest." I am a member of the Longshore Jobs Defense Committee of the Workers Defense League and, along with most of the other committee members, defendant in a libel action brought by Bridges for $250,000.

civil liberties, I am not for a moment suggesting that civil rights are unimportant.) In order to get an overview of the state of freedom within the unions today it is necessary to understand why the law had thus failed to deliver.

Under Title I of the Act, the union member's rights to democratic procedures are protected.[9] This portion of the law is enforced by the private suit of the aggrieved party. In effect, this limits the coverage of the statute to the militant oppositionist who cares enough about union politics to take his convictions to court. Title III of Landrum-Griffin, which deals with union trusteeships, is to be carried out either by the individual or by the action of the Department of Labor (this is an improvement but, as will be seen in a moment, it is also problematical).

Under this first section of the law, the individual member is given a legal right to publish handbills, distribute literature, hold caucus meetings, and mail letters to other unionists. These are, as H. W. Benson has pointed out, *individual* rights which, if protected, can be exercised independently of what the union does. The courts, Benson continues, have strongly supported these individual rights. In *Salzhandler* v. *Caputo,* the U.S. Court of Appeals for the Second Circuit upheld the right of members to criticize officials, even unjustifiably, and said that the unionists could not be tried within their unions on charges of slander.

However, there are other crucial rights which cannot be exercised independently of the union. In order for the democratic process to work, the organization itself must schedule meetings, hold referendums, provide time for discussion on

[9] A great deal of the factual material, and some of the analysis, in this account of the administration of the Landrum-Griffin law is taken from an unpublished manuscript, "Union Democracy, the Law, and the ACLU," prepared as a memo for the Civil Liberties Union in January, 1966, by H. W. Benson. As editor of *Union Democracy in Action,* Benson is one of the most informed and committed Americans concerned with this area. Although I have drawn heavily on both his published and unpublished materials, I alone am, of course, responsible for the conclusions which I have drawn.

the agenda, and establish procedures for the election of delegates, officers, and committeemen. The section of the law which deals most clearly with this area is 101 (a) (1), the "Equal Rights" provision. In *Calhoon* v. *Harvey*, the United States Supreme Court made an extremely restrictive interpretation of this portion of the law. A union member had brought suit in federal court alleging that his right to nominate, which is supposed to be protected under Title I, had been violated. The Court held that his complaint did not come under Title I and said of the equal rights provision:

> Plainly, this is no more than a command that members and classes of members shall not be discriminated against in the right to nominate and vote . . . . Whether the eligibility requirements set by the union's constitution and by-laws were reasonable and valid is a question separate and distinct from whether the right to nominate on an equal basis given by 101 (a) (1) has been violated.

The Court held that Title I does not really protect fair elections but only requires that all members be treated "equally"; that all rights pertaining to union elections are therefore enforceable only under Title IV of the law; that as a consequence, the Secretary of Labor must act to protect these rights (private individual suits are not authorized under Title IV; the Secretary is the only enforcement agency). So it was that part of the statute which spoke most broadly about membership freedoms was given a very limited scope and basic organizational rights were made dependent on the Department of Labor.

On the whole, the Department of Labor has been extremely prudent in its enforcement of these Title IV rights. Perhaps the most important single reason for this fact is that the Department was put in an impossible position by the law. Historically, the Labor Department had its origins in the theory that the basic interest groups in the country should have their "own" cabinet representation. The Department of Labor thus has a special relationship to organized workers, just as the

Department of Commerce has to business and the Department of Agriculture has to the organized farmers. Moreover, a great deal of the Department's dealing with the unions are cooperative in nature and, particularly under Democratic administrations since the New Deal, there is a tradition that the Secretary be acceptable to the union leadership.

It was foolish to think that a department with this special, and political, relationship to the labor movement could become a crusading agency which would, on the one hand, severely discipline the very same people who, on the other hand, were its most important constituents. Given the facts of Washington life, it was inevitable that the Department would take up its new responsibilities with considerable caution (it did so, incidentally, under the Republicans in 1959–60 as well as under the Democrats since 1960). One might imagine what would happen if the Department of Commerce were charged with forcing business compliance with minimum-wage laws or if the Department of Agriculture were required to investigate the bureaucratic practices of the Farm Bureau.

In 1963 Sam Denov, a candidate for office in Chicago Local 10 of the American Federation of Musicians, charged that his local election had been conducted illegally. The Department of Labor replied:

> The investigation disclosed evidence of violations of the Act in that the union failed to provide adequate safeguards to insure a fair election in failing to maintain an accurate count of the ballots printed, failing to count the unused ballots, and failing to properly safeguard the ballots cast . . . . Moreover, the union destroyed unused ballots in violation of Section 401 (c) . . . . *However, there is not probable cause to believe the violations found may have affected the election outcome; therefore, the case has been closed.* [Emphasis added.]

In such a reading of the law, it is possible for a bureaucracy to disarm and demoralize a democratic opposition through a whole series of sharp practices but then to escape censure (and an enforced change of policy) on the narrow grounds that the outcome of a particular election was not affected. Democracy can be subverted, but so long as this does not take the form of affecting the result (and since the ballots in Chicago were destroyed, it is hard to know how the Department came to its conclusion) that is legal.

Moreover, the Department, following the Supreme Court's logic in *Calhoon* v. *Harvey*, has restricted its activities under Title IV to *completed* elections. This means that the member has no legal recourse until his rights are fully and finally violated.

So as a result of court rulings and administrative discretion, the bold statement of membership rights contained in Landrum-Griffin have been narrowly restricted. It is possible that Department of Labor action growing out of the current dispute within the NMU will change this pattern (the Government is acting on the grounds that the conditions under which the election was held are in conflict with the statute). But as of now, it is the judicial and departmental history just described which has permitted attacks on internal democracy to continue within the labor movement.

So the reality since 1959 is complex. On the one hand the sweeping promises of the "Bill of Rights" advocates (and I am here talking of the sincere partisans of the Title and not of those reactionaries who used it as a means of attacking trade unionism itself) have not been fulfilled for the reasons just noted. There is therefore a need for further reform. But on the other hand, the myth of union tyranny perpetrated by the Right has been refuted in a great number of important cases by the democratic vitality of the unions themselves.

In theory, all Americans—trade unionists, union leaders, business, the public, and government—should be concerned about the civil liberties issues within the labor movement which have just been defined. In practice and despite all the pious rhetoric, most Americans either oppose or are indifferent to the issue. And this cynical fact must be described before it is possible to proceed to a discussion of what must be done.

To hear American businessmen talk, one would often think that they lose sleep over the fate of freedom within the unions. In fact, most executives do not want to deal with a vibrant, democratic union in which there is constant opposition and change, for both the ins and the outs will inevitably stake their claim to leadership on the basis of their ability to get a bigger settlement from the company. In some cases, the front office has simply tried to corrupt labor officials. More often, corporate power is used to promote "responsible" unionism. Seymour Martin Lipsett has said:

> There is a basic conflict between democratic unionism and "responsible" unionism, which many conservatives and business leaders do not recognize, at least in their public pronouncements.[10]

Perhaps the most extreme form of this contradiction was discovered by Frederic Meyers in Texas in the late fifties.[11] Meyers found businessmen who were passionate advocates of the state's right-to-work law and who had contributed money to get it passed but who nevertheless cheerfully and regularly cooperated with union leaders to run a *de facto* closed shop. After all, they said, that was the only way that management could get workers on a regular basis.

As a generalization, then, businessmen regularly prefer conservative, lethargic unions to dynamic ones.

Both the public and the government are rhetorically committed to civil liberties within labor organizations. But here again there is much more rhetoric than substance. When, in the summer of 1966, the rank-and-file members of the International Association of Machinists availed themselves of their statutory rights and rejected a contract their leaders had negotiated with the airlines, the air was literally filled with the

[10] "The Political Process in Trade Unions; A Theoretical Statement," in *Labor and Trade Unionism*, Walter Galenson and Seymour Lipsett eds. John Wiley, New York, 1960, p. 217.
[11] *Right-to-Work in Practice*, Fund for the Republic, New York, 1959.

outraged cries of the conservative champions of workers' freedom. *The New York Times* even suggested that the rightist congressional partisans of more democracy within the unions were now having second thoughts. They had intended the law to facilitate the mythic hatred of the members for their union leaders—and not as a means of expressing democratic militancy.

It is simply not rational to look to union leadership itself for a vigorous attack on its own powers. As Gus Tyler put it in *The Labor Revolution,*

> Labor leadership would like to believe that, left to itself, it would guarantee the members' rights and maintain a viable system of decision-making by the members. Some sophisticated leaders, with a genuine commitment to the democratic ideal, have set examples of self-restraint in the exercise of power. But the weight of the evidence indicates that in unions—as in business, government or driving a car—self-regulation is severely limited by the foibles and vanity of man.[12]

Finally, the members of unions themselves are not, under ordinary conditions, concerned with union democracy, and this is the most serious difficulty of all. As long as a leadership delivers on the bread-and-butter issues in a contract, most rank-and-filers will ignore their local meetings. Indeed, it is now a deep tradition within the labor movement that the members only turn out for strike and ratification votes. So it is possible for a local to have a constitution with a considerably undemocratic potential and yet not engage in any antidemocratic acts.[13]

Under such circumstances, the members might suddenly wake up one day to discover that they have been cheated of their rights and that there is nothing they can do about it; or else, they might spend their entire life in the organizations

[12] Gus Tyler, *op. cit. supra,* p. 243.
[13] See my book, *The Retail Clerks,* John Wiley & Sons, New York, 1962, Chapter VI, for a case in point.

without realizing the existence of a threat to their freedom. Two contrasting tendencies affect this fact of membership apathy. As the nation becomes more affluent and as the wages of the organized labor force increase, the importance of the union in the life of the worker declines somewhat. In earlier and poorer days, the job was the absolute center of a man's life and the American unions fought more militantly and violently on this issue than any other labor organization in the world. It was in this phase of its existence that labor appeared as a "movement" and not just as an organization. Most classically in the social democratic unions of Europe, but in the United States as well, working-class institutions were social, cultural, and intellectual centers for their members as well as agencies for collective bargaining.

Now, however, a man works much shorter hours and has the money to indulge in a variety of leisure-time activities. (I am obviously speaking of the organized workers here, most of whom are in a vastly superior economic position compared to the poor. Indeed, one of the reasons that the poor are poor is that they have been denied the advantages of trade union organization.) The union then becomes one activity among many rather than a comprehensive movement. And it is under such circumstances that indifference can become institutionalized so long as the leadership wins steady advances. And even though the union constitution may be structurally deficient, the worker simply does not care.

But, on the other hand, there is the evidence noted by *The Wall Street Journal* that in the affluent America of 1966–67 with unemployment at the lowest level in a decade there has been a wave of rank-and-file militancy. In part, this represents the impatience of younger workers; in part, it represents a consciousness that the rate of business profits improved much faster than labor wages in the recent past. In any case, the existence of such a trend is one of the most optimistic factors, from the point of view of union democracy, in the labor movement today.

However, it would be wrong to conclude this section on

such a hopeful note. For the fact of the matter is that
management, the public, the government, the labor leadership, and the rank and file are often hostile to, or apathetic
about, freedom within unions. And despite all the ringing
affirmations which one hears about defending the civil liberties of workers within their own organizations, there are few
who take the issue as seriously as it deserves. And the experiences of 1966 and 1967, when the membership has proved
much more militant on economic issues than the leaders, may
well cause conservatives who thought expanding rights would
help them in their fight against unionism to reverse their cynical strategy and call for restrictions upon the membership.

Given all of these problematic aspects of the situation, the
political factors noted earlier become even more important. It
is not enough to develop an ideal system of labor liberties in
the abstract. In seeking reform, it is necessary to emphasize
those proposals which can actually win the support of a progressive majority. And this means, as I hope to show in a
moment, that the changes must have an appeal to the best of
the committed unionists themselves and that they cannot once
again seem to represent a hypocritical exercise in union busting on the part of the enemies of labor.

The aim of civil libertarian reform in the American labor
movement can be simply put: within his own union, the
worker must be guaranteed all of the freedoms which he
enjoys as a citizen under the Bill of Rights of the United
States Constitution.

It is certainly true, as Arthur Goldberg and others have
argued, that there is no simple analogy between labor
organizations and the civil government. The fact that unions
have a "combat" function at the very center of their existence
does give them a unique quality. And yet, even though this
factor must be taken into account, the unions of the late
sixties are not underground groupings but major institutions
in the United States. Indeed, it is precisely in those organizations which are in the stage of life-and-death struggle, like the

migrant farm workers, that the issue of democracy hardly arises. For such sections of the movement are so dependent upon the solidarity of their members that a bureaucratic denial of freedom to the rank and file would destroy them.

So the problem really arises in the successful unions. There, negotiations have become so complex, contracts so intricate, that the individual needs due process protections just as he does in the society at large. There are, to be sure, still strike battles led by such organizations but it would be a denial of the magnificent accomplishment of the labor movement itself to take these as the defining fact of their existence. So with all due care—*toutes proportions gardées*—one can assert that the members of unions must enjoy civil liberties analogous to the citizen of the society.

The most hopeful means of protecting the democratic rights of workers is not to be found in the Landrum-Griffin Act. Rather, it was invented by trade unionists themselves in the United Automobile Workers. It is the institution of the public review board. In what follows, I am primarily concerned with public review as it relates to the labor movement. However, the principle which it embodies is so important that I believe it should be extended to every major organization in the land.[14]

Under public review, a member who has a grievance against the union because of the denial of his rights first seeks to process his claim through the normal appeal mechanism. When he has stated his case before the local and the International Executive Board, he has a choice. At that point, he can either appeal to the union convention or to the Review Board. The latter is composed of prominent citizens, none of whom may have any relationship with the union. Under the UAW procedures, the Review Board has the right to overrule the International Executive Board (the Review Board of the

---

[14] For an early description of the UAW Review Board, *cf. Democracy and Public Review*, by Jack Stieber, Walter E. Oberer, and Michael Harrington, Fund for the Republic, Santa Barbara, 1960. For the larger implications of the review principle see my *Toward a Democratic Left*, Macmillan, New York, 1968, Chapter VI.

American Federation of Teachers has a similar jurisdiction; the boards of the Packinghouse and Upholsterers unions are much more limited in scope).

One of the first consequences of the UAW Review Board was to promote a vast increase in *voluntary* due process within the union. That is, local officials were reminded that every one of their actions might be scrutinized by an independent board. In order to avoid embarrassing reversals, they became more careful in their use of the union's disciplinary machinery. Indeed, there were those on the Review Board itself who felt that the ultimate proof of their efficacy would come on the day when there were no cases to handle.

A recent case demonstrates what public review means in the UAW.

In May, 1965, ballots were counted in the election for Financial Secretary of Local 36. An independent CPA firm reported that Frank O'Hara had polled 1,500 votes and Frank Cristiano 1,439; and 326 ballots were not marked for any candidate for the post. Cristiano and other defeated candidates demanded a recount but the CPA firm refused to go on with the procedure when scores of unmarked ballots later turned out to be marked for Cristiano. The Local Election Committee demanded that the recount continue and the final results increased Cristiano's tally by 114 and O'Hara's by 4. The CPA firm would not certify this tally. However, the Committee declared Cristiano elected.

O'Hara appealed to the UAW Executive Board which was quite prepared to admit that the whole affair looked quite suspicious and ordered a new election. O'Hara did not accept this ruling since he believed that he had won the first election fair and square and should not be required to take his chances in a second vote. The Review Board responded to his appeal by ruling:

> We agree with appellant O'Hara that since there was no evidence indicating anything wrong with the initial count, he is entitled to be declared the elected Financial

Secretary of the Local without the necessity of having to stand for election a second time . . . . Were we to direct a new election, we would be saying in effect that those who benefit from the alteration of the ballot could profit from the wrongdoing obvious in the circumstances of this case.

Now it must be frankly stated that there are not many unions which will voluntarily surrender as much sovereignty as the UAW has. Allowing nonmembers to rule on an election and overturn the union's highest body is a remarkable grant of authority. Since the UAW constituted its Board, many reformers have proposed that this approach be taken up by the entire labor movement. The suggestion has been rebuffed in almost every case. In fairness, it must be said that the notion of giving such power to "outsiders" goes against the grain of the American labor tradition and even raises some difficult questions for democratic theory. And yet, there is no single reform which could accomplish so much in guaranteeing civil liberties throughout the labor movement than the review board.

For this reason, I would make the encouragement of the creation of genuine review boards the main focus of legislative strategy. And I think this can be done in such a way as to enlist the greatest possible sympathy from the labor movement itself.

As the preceding analysis has made clear, the Landrum-Griffin Act failed in its announced intentions of guaranteeing basic freedoms to the members of unions. In part this was because of the actual deficienceis in the legislation, or in the judicial and administrative interpretarions of it, that have been already described. In part, it was an almost inevitable consequence of the political history of Landrum-Griffin, which predisposed large segments of the labor movement to suspect every effort to enforce the law as one more expression of the antiunion attitudes of its framers. If there is to be meaningful progress in this area, both of these pitfalls must be avoided.

That is, there must be an effective law which is not violently opposed by the majority of trade union officials. It is, to put it mildly, difficult to suggest a statute which will meet this criterion but there is one approach which might work.

First of all, there must be a clear legislative statement of the rights of the worker. The enforcement of such a provision should be assigned to an independent agency on the order of the National Labor Relations Board. In all cases involving democratic freedoms, there should be a place for both governmental and individual litigation. And all of the antilibertarian features of Landrum-Griffin—the detailed specification of how dues are to be increased in which the Congress arrogated to itself a decision which belongs to the rank and file; the sections depriving alleged Communists and former criminals of rights; and so on—should be repealed.

*There should then be a mechanism which would allow any union to gain almost total exemption from the Act.* If a union would voluntarily meet the minimum standards of democracy defined by the law in its constitution and would provide a genuine review board to enforce this commitment, then it would only be subjected to a periodic check to be sure that it was living up to these guarantees (review boards, after all, could be stacked). If it turned out that the review principle was being manipulated for antidemocratic purposes, the union would then come under the most stringent supervision in the law. But so long as it provided genuine review protections it would in effect be free from any federal intervention.

Now this notion of a "reserved powers" approach has been suggested before and it did not excite great support among the labor leadership. Moreover, the impetus for reform which culminated in Landrum-Griffin was partly a consequence of senatorial investigations of James Hoffa and the Teamsters Union, and partly a tactic of the antilaborites. And it is difficult to imagine the circumstances in which the opportunity for change would arrive under progressive auspices. Therefore, the legal encouragement of the review approach is not put forward here as a magic panacea. It is urged as the best way

available to make it plain that the intent of civil libertarians
in this area is not to punish the labor movement for real or
imagined sins, but to cooperate with it in helping it to live up
to its own high ideals.

There is one hopeful trend which could make this tactic
more realistic. In recent years, the changing nature of American technology has altered the shape of the work force and
the composition of the union membership. The craft skills
show a declining rate of increase; the semi-skilled occupations
organized by the industrial unions required a boom to reach
their 1955 levels; and there has been a vast surge of service
employments, particularly in health services and education.
And all of the figures show that these tendencies will continue
into the foreseeable future.

The most spectacular gains in union membership have
taken place in the new service fields, most dramatically in the
rise of the American Federation of Teachers. This is extremely
important from the point of view of union democracy since
most of the sociological evidence indicates that civil libertar-
ianism is an "educated" position; i.e., in the secure middle
class with its Marquis of Queensberry rules, there is more tol-
erance for an opponent's right to speak than at the rough-and-
tumble levels of the society. So if manpower trends are increasing the educational level of the labor movement, they
may also be broadening the membership base which supports
public review. Significantly, the AFT does have an excellent
review mechanism.

And yet, I do not want to rest my case on some sort of snob
notion that the unions can only become democratic if they
take off the blue work shirts. For the workingmen and work-
ingwomen of America have made, and are making, an enormous contribution to the democratic vitality of their country.
Indeed, I would argue that the unions have done more
to extend the range of freedom in America than any other
voluntary institution. In the post-World War II period, the
leaders of the reform drive were, more often than not, those
who had fought labor at its very best. As a result of this cyni-

cal political fact, the union leadership responded negatively to any and all proposals for legislative reform which required federal intervention.

Yet the evidence indicates that, in a limited but glaring number of cases, rank-and-filers are still denied democratic freedoms. It also shows that there is an extraordinary amount of effective democracy within the movement. It is for this reason that proposals to deal with the remaining evils should be designed to encourage the very real internal vitality which does exist. And it is from this perspective that I suggest that a "reserved powers" approach to public review would help the largest nongovernmental democratic institution in the society to fulfill its functions even more effectively than ever before.

# About the Contributors

John de J. Pemberton, Jr., a former professor of law at Duke University, practiced law in Rochester, Minnesota, before becoming the executive director of the American Civil Liberties Union in 1962.

Harriet F. Pilpel is one of the nation's leading communications attorneys, and serves as chairman of the Committee on Communications Media of the American Civil Liberties Union and is a member of its Board of Directors. She is also a leader in the birth control and abortion-reform movements.

Walter Millis was an editorial writer for *The New York Herald Tribune* for thirty years and developed an expertise in military affairs. Editor of *The Forrestal Papers*, he authored nine other major works, including *Why Europe Fights* (1940) and *Arms and Men* (1956). At the time of his death in early 1968 he was on the staff of the Center for the Study of Democratic Institutions, and also served as a member of the Board of Directors of the American Civil Liberties Union.

Robert Bierstedt is professor of sociology at New York University, and was formerly the head of that department. A member of the Board of Directors of the American Civil Liberties Union, he served as chairman of the Academic Freedom Committee and now heads its Church-State Committee.

Louis M. Hacker, a professor of economics at Columbia University, was formerly Dean of the School of General Studies at Columbia. An expert in economic history, he has edited and authored more than fifteen books. One of the early leaders for student academic freedom, he served for ten years as chairman of the Academic Freedom Committee of the American Civil Liberties Union and wrote several of the Committee's policy statements and pamphlets. He is now a member of the Board of Directors of the American Civil Liberties Union.

Elmer Rice, a Pulitzer Prize-winning playwright, was recognized as one of the major figures in the American theater. He was a member of the Board of Directors of the American Civil Liberties Union for thirty-four years, until his death in 1967. His inveterate opposition to censorship took form within the ACLU by his chairing of its National Council on Freedom from Censorship in the 1940's and 1950's and later on of its Censorship Committee.

Edward J. Ennis, a member of the Board of Directors of the American Civil Liberties Union since 1946, has served as its general counsel since 1954. He practices law in New York City. In World War II he held a key post in the Department of Justice.

Osmond K. Fraenkel is regarded as one of the nation's leading constitutional authorities. His analyses and descriptions of Supreme Court decisions, collected in *The Supreme Court and Civil Liberties,* has been widely praised by practicing attorneys and laymen alike. A member of the Board of Directors of the American Civil Liberties Union since 1935, he was named general counsel in 1954, a post he still holds.

Loren Miller, until his death in 1967, was a towering legal figure in the Negro people's struggle to achieve their rights. An eloquent writer as well as an attorney, Mr. Miller piloted many pace-making cases through the courts that broke housing discrimination and other barriers. A member of the National Committee of the American Civil Liberties Union, at the time of his death Mr. Miller was a judge of the municipal court in Los Angeles.

Michael Harrington is an internationally known writer and crusader for social justice. His *The Other America* is credited with being the initial stimulus for turning the nation's and the government's attention to the problems of the poor. An experienced student of the labor movement, Mr. Harrington has written frequently on the status of democracy within unions. A former member of the ACLU Board of Directors, he is chairman of the League for Industrial Democracy.

Alan Reitman has been a member of the staff of the American Civil Liberties Union since 1949, and its associate director for the past ten years. He is the author of numerous magazine articles on civil liberties subjects. He is a public affairs expert, particularly in those areas relating to human rights and social action. Before joining the ACLU staff, he was Director of Public Relations of the CIO Political Action Committee and Assistant Director of Public Relations at Rutgers University.

# Index

239